The Wonder Series

Eagles

Hunters of the Sky

Written
by
Ann C. Cooper

Designed and Illustrated
by
Gail Kohler Opsahl
and
Marjorie C. Leggitt

Denver Museum of Natural History
and Roberts Rinehart Publishers

Published in the United States of America
by Roberts Rinehart Publishers
Post Office Box 666,
Niwot, Colorado 80544

Published in Great Britain, Ireland,
and Europe by
Roberts Rinehart Publishers,
3 Bayview Terrace, Schull, West Cork
Republic of Ireland

Published in Canada by Key Porter Books,
70 The Esplanade, Toronto,
Ontario M5E 1R2

Library of Congress Catalog Card Number
91-066681

International Standard Book Number
1-879373-11-4

Manufactured in the
United States of America

Many people contributed to *Eagles: Hunters of the Sky*, by sharing their expertise on eagles, reviewing the text for accuracy, and enriching the material with their personal experiences: Dr. Charles Preston, Joyce Herold, Diana Lee Crew, and Leslie Newell of the Denver Museum of Natural History; Mike Lockhart and Carol Ann Moorhead from the U.S. Fish and Wildlife Service at the Rocky Mountain Arsenal; John Wright from Shell; Jerry Craig, Colorado Division of Wildlife; Karen Steenhof, Snake River Birds of Prey Research Project, Bureau of Land Management; Dr. Gary Bortolotti, University of Saskatchewan.

Sigrid Ueblacker of the Birds of Prey Rehabilitation Foundation, Broomfield, Colorado, graciously provided information and hands-on demonstration of the rehabilitation of raptors. Gene Poor Bear and his son, Michael, assisted with American Indian aspects of the book. Michael posed for the drawings in the story and in his eagle-feathered powwow clothes. Gene also assisted with the Lakota words, as did Violet Catches and Dr. David Rood. Lucille Echohawk reviewed the story.

Fifth grade students from Crestview Elementary School, Boulder, and Mrs. Sandstrom, their teacher, shared what they knew and what they wanted to learn about eagles.

I wish to thank them all.

—Ann C. Cooper

Eagles
Hunters of the Sky

Contents

Introduction

Think of an eagle...

Did you think first of a Bald Eagle, the national bird of the United States? The Bald Eagle, with its bright white head and its fierce unblinking gaze, is the only eagle that lives exclusively in North America. In 1782, the Bald Eagle was chosen as our emblem. The eagle represents pride and strength— qualities we want for our country.

Did you think first of North America's other eagle, the Golden Eagle? The Golden Eagle deserves its nickname, "king of birds." It, too, is strong and fierce-looking. It is called golden because of the gleaming golden feathers on the back of the neck of an adult bird.

Or did you think of another kind of eagle? Each person reading this book has different ideas, images, or memories of eagles based on his or her experience of eagles.

3

Background to the Story

The story that follows is about Bald Eagles and a city boy who develops a new pride in himself and the ways of his people in his "Summer of the Eagle."

Although this story is fictitious, the idea for it came from a real Bald Eagle nest at Barr Lake State Park near Denver, Colorado. The boy is Sioux, and the story borrows ideas and feelings from the Sioux, one of the nations of American Indian people.

The Sioux first began to move into the Great Plains around 1750. Before then, they had hunted and fished near the Mississippi River in the area that is now southern Minnesota, Wisconsin, and northern Iowa.

After their migration, they became plains hunters. Their way of life centered around the great herds of bison. They understood the land and its changing moods and seasons. The sun, moon, and stars were their guides. Summers they spent on the hunt. In October, the Moon of Changing Seasons, thoughts turned to sheltered winter camps. The Sioux had great reverence for all living things, the four-legged, the two-legged, the winged, and those that slithered or crawled. They used what they needed from the land but did not waste plants or animals. Though they hunted the bison, they always gave a part back to the land as a symbol of their respect for all life.

The Sioux, like all American Indian people, revered eagles for their qualities of strength, pride, and independence. They believed that the eagle was close to the Great Mystery, or Creator. The eagle could fly high into the skies, yet it had chosen to live on earth. Surely, they thought, it must be a messenger from the spirit world. Eagle feathers were important symbols in the way of life of the Sioux.

Nowadays, eagle feathers may be used only with special permission. It is against federal and state laws to harm an eagle. If eagles are accidentally killed or are found dead, their bodies are sent to a special department of the United States Fish and Wildlife Service. American Indians may apply for permits to get feathers for cultural purposes. No one else is allowed to obtain them, unless it is for serious scientific purposes. Special laws have been passed to protect eagles and other birds of prey so they will continue to be part of our living heritage.

Pronunciation Guide

Some of the words used in the story come from the language of the Teton Sioux—Lakota.

tonweya (tuhn-WEE-uh): guide

wag a chun (WAH ha chuh): cottonwood tree

Wakan Tanka (wah-KUHN TAHN-kuh): Great Spirit, or Creator

wanbli (wahm-BLEE): eagle

Summer of the Eagle

Gilbert One Feather never thought much about being Sioux or about the old ways being important—never, that is, until the summer of the eagle.

Of course, ever since he could remember, Gil had loved the times when Grandfather told stories to all the children. Sometimes the stories would be about when Grandfather was a boy—about finding deer fawns and hunting for nests. You could almost feel the silence and see the bright stars when Grandfather told about the Great Horned Owls that hunted so quietly they were no more than a whispered breath in the night. Grandfather always talked about "home" as if home was still in Pine Ridge, near the Black Hills, even though he had lived in Denver for years and years. Sometimes he sounded sad for home and for the past.

Other times, but not often, the children would persuade Grandfather to talk about "The War," when he was a true warrior. Grandfather had fought overseas and had won a medal for bravery. But he said he was prouder of his eagle feathers than of his medal because the eagle feathers were the *true* signs of courage.

Most of all, Gil liked the stories from long ago. "Did I ever tell you...," Grandfather would begin, and they would all settle around him, knowing a good story was coming. Gil's favorite was the one about *Tonweya**, who climbed down into the eagle's eyrie on a rawhide rope. Gil had never seen an eagle, or an eagle's eyrie, except in pictures. But in his imagination he could see Tonweya sitting with the eaglets after his rope came untied from the tree at the top of the cliff. He could picture Tonweya stranded with no food and getting thinner and thinner. He could picture the eaglets getting fatter and fatter, stronger and stronger, as Tonweya fed them pieces of rawhide. And Gil would hold his breath when the time came for Tonweya to fly to the ground below the cliff by holding an eagle in each hand. Of course, you couldn't really fly like that! But it was a great story.

They were all great stories. But for Gil, they didn't have much to do with his everyday life. Stories were for kids, and now that Gil was twelve, he had other things to think about.

He had other things to worry about...

Things like a best friend moving away and wrecking all the plans for a whole summer...

Things like finding a great hole in the ground where the hideout used to be...

* The story of Tonweya is taken from *Tonweya and the Eagles and Other Lakota Indian Tales* by Rosebud Yellow Robe, published by Dial Press, New York. 1979.

The hideout, a vacant lot that was overgrown and tangly with weeds, had been Gil's secret place for years. Someone had abandoned an old chair there, still comfortable in spite of its popping springs. It was a good place to hang out with a friend or to get away by yourself when you had problems to work out.

But today, when Gil got there, he almost thought he'd turned into the wrong street. They'd surrounded the lot with a six-foot chain-link fence that had three strands of barbed wire leaning out at an angle from the top. Instead of the weeds there was a huge rectangular hole. The chair was tipped on one side and half-covered with dirt. A large red sign said

Danger
Keep Out
Construction Zone

Changes, changes, changes. Sometimes Gil thought the city was trying to squeeze out the people. They kept building tall towers, full of reflecting glass, that seemed to lean in on the streets as if they were falling. Every little space in the whole city was getting filled up. And now his secret place was nothing but an enormous hole waiting to sprout a concrete giant. Gil kicked angrily at the fencing, then walked home.

"Why the gloomy face?" Gil's grandfather asked, as soon as Gil walked in the door.

"I hate everything," Gil said. "Why do things have to change?"

"What's changing?" Grandfather said.

"Everything," Gil said angrily, as he slammed the door shut. "My secret place is gone. Dug up. Fenced. But I don't suppose it matters. I won't need a secret place anymore because my friend is moving away."

"Ah! I understand. Your place is gone! Your friend is moving on and you can't let him go," Grandfather said.

Gil could sense a lecture coming. Grandfather was fixing a thong on one of the eagle feathers on his war bonnet. Gil had noticed before that Grandfather often started talking about serious stuff—what Gil called "talking deep"—when he was working on his outfit. It was as if the clothes made Grandfather think of the old ways.

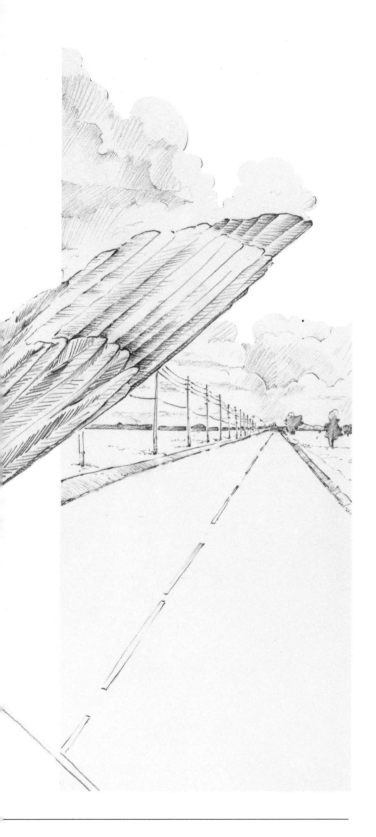

"Things are always changing, always moving on," Grandfather began in his lecture voice. "Remember what our people say. To live right with yourself, and with all people, you can't hold on to things too hard. You can't own friends or places. All you can do is share in another life for a while, and then wish a friend a good road to travel. All you can do is borrow a little piece of Earth for a moment of time. You have to give freely, be generous, and only then will everything return to you."

"Courage isn't just bravery in war," Grandfather went on, more softly now. "It isn't just an eagle feather for a brave deed. Courage is being alone and not afraid. It's letting go. It's running to welcome the future because life is sweet. There are things I must show you. Tomorrow we will go discover them together."

Grandfather and Gil set out early next morning to go to the big reservoir east of the city. It was to be their day together. Gil knew that if anything could make up for missing a friend, this day would.

The cottonwoods—Grandfather said they were called *wag a chun*, the rustling trees—were like shimmering cascades of apple-green against the blue sky. Their leafy reflections danced in the slight ripples of the clear water. A damp and musty fragrance, part earth and part honey, filled the air. The morning was noisy with a thousand different songs and calls, clicks, croaks, and chirrups. Grandfather seemed to know all the voices as if they were old friends.

"Hear the one saying 'wichety, wichety, wichety'? That's the little yellowthroat warbler down in the reeds," Grandfather said. "The one that sounds as if it needs oiling—why that's the old blackbird with the yellow head." Grandfather laughed a deep laugh. "This is the sweet life. Didn't I tell you! It all works together. It all belongs. And we do too. Even if we're stuck for a while in the city, this must be a part of our spirit. Birds, fishes, bugs—what a great circle of life keeps us company today!"

Just then a shadow swept across the sunny grasses. The birds fell silent.

10

"Grandfather! Look up! It's huge!" Gil's words tumbled out over each other in his rush to show Grandfather the very largest bird he had ever seen. "Is it an eagle? Don't eagles live in faraway wild places? I wish it could be an eagle! It looks as if it is carrying something."

"It's hard to see against the light, but I see a white head, white tail, and a good-sized fish to take home," Grandfather said. "We call him *wanbli*, eagle, spirit messenger…." Grandfather sighed and rested his arm over Gil's shoulders. "Yes, Gil, it's a Bald Eagle—and it's going home."

The nest was high in one of the tallest rustling trees. To one side of it a silver-white bare branch stuck skyward. Gil was sure another eagle was perched on the branch. And he could see two fuzzy-looking white blobs showing above the enormous stick nest.

"I wish we could get closer," Gil said.

"That wouldn't do," Grandfather said. "Eagles need their space. It's lucky there is a deep channel. That should keep the nest safe from curious people."

"Are the blobs babies?" Gil asked.

"Eaglets," Grandfather said. "Two of them. Must be plenty of food for the taking this year."

Gil came back to see the eagles time and again in the next days and weeks. He fixed up his bike to make the long ride, and he spent all his free moments watching from a distance as the young ones, darker colored now, began exercising their wings and even trying short play-flights above the nest. It was as if by watching the eagles, Gil learned a whole new way of looking. He started to see all the other alive-ones, too. One day a bull snake slithered over his sneaker and disappeared into the weeds. Another day he watched four gaping woodpecker beaks poking out of a tree hole as a parent bird swooped in with a beak full of grubs. Here—close to the city, with airplanes overhead, and clusters of city houses pushing and shoving into the ranch land—even here, Gil felt a thousand miles away. Life was sweet in this magical place. He hoped the eagles would never get squeezed out.

Nothing prepared him for disaster.

He could tell the eaglets were gone—they must have flown. That was the way it had to be. He searched the skies. High above, outlined against billowing storm clouds, he could see tiny specks of dark. There were only three of them.

On this side of the channel, something that looked like a rag lay in the grass. Gil's heart lurched, then began to thump so violently it felt as if his ribs would explode. He felt sick and shaky with dread. Please no! Please no! The half-thoughts raced through his mind as he ran toward the rag.

The "rag" was a pitiful heap of feathers with a streak of blood across one wing. But alive. His eagle! His Shining One!

Afterward Gil could only vaguely remember the journey home. Had he really shouted for Grandfather from the end of the street? Or had Grandfather already been coming to meet him as if he had had a premonition?

Gil knew he must have told Grandfather about the hurt eagle but he couldn't recall the words. All he could remember was climbing into the truck and Grandfather driving back to the eagle, so fast that Gil had expected to hear sirens. When they got there, the eagle was still alive, fluttering slightly, and panting. Its eyes looked wild. Grandfather gently covered its head with a cloth to quiet it. He held the eagle's legs so it could not strike and folded the wings. The eagle was too weak to protest. Together Gil and Grandfather wrapped the bird in Gil's denim jacket. And Gil cradled the eagle in his arms as they piled into their pick-up truck. The truck became an eagle ambulance, rushing toward the raptor rehabilitation hospital that Grandfather knew about.

13

Gil felt a knot of panic as he watched the veterinarian examine his eagle.

"Well, it's a female…not in bad shape, considering…." the vet said. "We check for emaciation, that's how thin she is, by feeling here." The vet's fingers probed the eagle's breast muscles gently. "The x-ray we took showed that she's got a shotgun pellet in the left wing. We'll leave it in—that often does less damage to flight muscles than poking around trying to remove it. She's lost a feather or two, and this one is so loose it's falling out." The vet gently removed the feather.

"Will she be able to fly again?" Gil asked. He crossed his fingers, wishing hard for the answer he hoped to hear.

"I don't see why not, if all goes well," the vet said. "The pellet will become enclosed almost like a pearl forms around a grain of sand. We'll keep your Shining One in intensive care for a while—make sure she doesn't go into shock. Did you report this to the authorities?"

"We wanted to get the eagle here quickly, we didn't take time to think about reporting…" Grandfather said.

"I'll call the United States Fish and Wildlife officer right now," the vet said. "You're American Indian, aren't you Gil? I'll see if I can get permission for you to keep the feather that fell out. I know eagle feathers have special meaning for you."

14

Later, in the truck going home, Gil smoothed the feather that the vet had given him. He felt a surge of black anger as he thought again of Shining One's battered wing.

"Grandfather, why would anyone shoot an eagle?"

"Some people are ignorant or thoughtless. They forget that it takes many ages to create and only seconds to destroy," Grandfather replied softly. "We all need to understand that a world that is not safe for eagles is a world that is no good for people either."

Gil's Shining One needed care and tenderness while her wing gradually healed. For the rest of the summer Gil did his part to help, doing any odd jobs just so he could be there, close to Shining One. First, it was enough to know she was eating well. Then came the time for her to leave intensive care and move in with other eagles. Gil felt happy-sad that day—happy that Shining One was getting better, but sad to know that he must watch through a small peephole now, so that Shining One would not be disturbed by his presence. Shining One must learn eagle-stuff again and forget her meeting with humans. She must learn flying and hunting skills again. For Gil, the day that Shining One took a first wobbly flight on healing wings was better than any birthday. He felt warm inside to think he'd helped to make this possible.

15

September came, time for a new school with no best friend to share the scariness of the first day. Gil felt a few moments of panic. Then he thought of Shining One. She must have felt panic, too, but she'd survived her fear.

Now that Gil could only visit on Saturdays, he noticed changes in Shining One from week to week. She grew stronger. Her feathers were sleeker and glossier. She caught her own food—well, sometimes she scavenged bits of fish from the other eagles! She swooped from the ground to the high perch at the end of the long flight cage as if it cost her no effort at all.

Finally, by December, Shining One was well enough to fly free. Gil and Grandfather were there to watch her fly out from a bluff high above a silvery, snaking river. It was a place where many eagles gathered to spend the winter. The vet said it was a good place for Shining One to learn to be truly wild again. Grandfather said a prayer to *Wakan Tanka* that Shining One might have a good soaring wind and a safe path to travel. Gil knew that here was space enough for eagles away from the crowding city!

The cottonwood trees, their skeleton winter branches lightly dusted with sparkling snowflakes, stretched along the valley as far as he could see. And now Gil could see other eagles! Shining One was back in the wild with her own kind.

He knew he would probably never see Shining One again. But he had a gleaming feather by which to remember her—his first eagle feather earned for a brave deed, Grandfather said. There would be other eagles in his life. There *had* to be. And space for them, too. He'd make sure of that.

Gil wanted to shout and sing for joy and gratitude. He understood, now, what Grandfather had meant about sharing and letting go. For every end was also a beginning.

The End

(The Beginning...)

Afterword to the Story

On December 16, 1990, four Bald Eagles (Hope, Thunder, Spirit, and Hamlet) flew free after months of care at the Birds of Prey Rehabilitation Foundation, Broomfield, Colorado. Mr. Buddy Redbow, an Oglala Sioux, traveled from Pine Ridge, South Dakota, to be present at the release and to say a special prayer for the eagles.

Activities
with
Eagles

Sign of the Eagle

An eagle circles with effortless grace in a storm-cloud sky. It's a huge bird, but rising spirals take it higher and higher until it becomes a tiny, distant speck. What power and strength are in its wings. How free and independent the eagle looks as we watch from far below. No wonder people all over the world from the very earliest times respected, and even worshipped, this bird. No wonder the eagle became a symbol of power and pride.

As you read look for this sign to find out about eagle symbols in myth, folktales, history, and present times.

ROBERTS
RINEHART

ROBERTS RINEHART PUBLISHERS

PO BOX 666, Niwot, Colorado 80544-0666
TEL 303.530.4400   FAX 303.530.4488   rhinobooks@aol.com

To receive a free catalog of ROBERTS RINEHART books and audiotapes,
please return this card. Indicate your interests by checking below:

☐ Art & Photography   ☐ Irish Nonfiction
☐ Children   (politics, culture, history)
☐ Young Adult   ☐ Natural History/Nature
☐ History   ☐ American West
☐ Fiction   ☐ Travel

Name ....

Address ....

City .... State .... Zip ....

Title of this book: ....

Where purchased: ....

Comments: ....

ROBERTS
RINEHART

ROBERTS RINEHART PUBLISHERS

PO BOX 666
NIWOT CO 80544-0666

Place
Postage
Here

The Language of Feathers

Imagine you were an American Indian living hundreds of years ago. All your food, all your clothes, the home in which you lived, came from the land. You couldn't run to the corner store for groceries. A summer of drought or a severe winter could mean you'd go hungry.

That is why the people needed to know and understand the cycle of the seasons. They needed to know when to gather berries and where to go to collect special roots. They couldn't hunt unless they knew how to track deer and bison.

They believed that all living things had an important place in the great circle of life and that the people themselves were part of that circle, not set apart. Many of their prayers asked the help of spirits, animals, and birds—especially the eagle.

The eagle had power and strength. It hunted from the skies, seeing its prey from far away and swooping to kill with great skill. If only a person could share the power of the eagle by wearing parts of the eagle, then perhaps a warrior or hunter could be as strong as an eagle that circled high in the sky!

The Sioux used feathers from both Bald and Golden Eagles in their clothing and ceremonies, not simply for ornament but for their deeper meaning.

Look for the constellation that is called Aquila, the eagle, in the summer sky. The brightest star is Altair.

19

The eagle feather warbonnet was worn by great warriors. Each feather represented a deed of courage. The feathers were fastened by rawhide thongs in such a way that each feather moved as if mimicking the wingbeats of a live eagle.

Other warriors wore single eagle feathers, often cut in special ways to show how they had been earned. Even the angle at which the feather was worn had meaning to those who knew the language of the feathers. The feather was worn in the scalp lock (the hair growing from the crown of the head). It was believed that the feather would protect the wearer from harm.

Eagle dancers wore eagle feathers in their hair and carried fans made of eagle tails. Sixteen men took part in the eagle dance. They circled, four at a time, their steps echoing the movements of eagles.

The pipe, called a *calumet*, used in sacred ceremonies often had eagle feathers hanging from its stem. In fact, another name for the Golden Eagle is Calumet Bird. The eagle staff, the top of which was sometimes made from eagle talons or an eagle head had hanging feathers, too.

The Sioux people made whistles out of the leg bones of eagles. With these whistles, the Sioux made weird, hypnotic sounds for the Sundance, one of their most sacred ceremonies. The dancers clenched the whistles between their teeth so that each time they breathed out, the whistles wailed. These whistles worked because of the special structure of bird bones. Next time you eat chicken or turkey, try breaking or cutting a leg bone in half (ask a grown-up to help). What does it look like inside?

Nowadays, many traditions are celebrated at powwows. What is a powwow? It is a meeting, reunion, and festival all in one. Powwows are held in many places in North America. Dancers from all over the country come to perform their traditional dances and songs, and to compete for prizes in the dancing and singing.

The modern dancers wear beautiful outfits, designed to follow family and tribal traditions. Although historical outfits with real eagle feathers are treasured by their owners, many modern clothes have other kinds of feathers instead of the traditional eagle feathers.

Navaho people called the month of January "the time when eagles talk." At that time of year, Golden Eagles jabber and call during their courtship flights.

The Skies Belong to Eagles

What exactly *is* an eagle? In everyday language, eagles, the largest of the hawks, are birds of prey that hunt by day. They are also called **raptors**. The word raptor comes from a Latin word, *raptare*, which means "to seize and carry away."

Scientists give each **species** (kind) of living thing a two-part scientific name, so it won't be confused with any other species. While living things may have many common names, they only have one scientific name.

The Golden Eagle has different common names in different parts of the world. American War Bird, Black Eagle, Brown Eagle, Canadian Eagle, Calumet Bird, Royal Eagle, *Aguila real* (in Spanish), and Jackrabbit Eagle are a few of them. You can imagine that using common names could be very confusing. You'd never be sure that two people were talking about the same kind of bird. However, the Golden Eagle's scientific name is *Aquila chrysaetos*—anywhere in the world.

The first part of the name refers to the **genus**. Some other eagles beside the Golden Eagle are in the genus *Aquila*. All the eagles in that genus have some features similar to the Golden Eagle. The second part of the name, *chrysaetos* (meaning golden) is unique to the Golden Eagle.

Similar species are grouped together in a genus. In the same way scientists group similar **genera** (more than one genus) together in a **family**. Most scientists believe that 22 genera that include 59 species worldwide should be classified as eagles. They are grouped into the family *Accipitridae*, along with the ospreys, hawks, kites, and old world vultures.

Eagles inhabit every continent except Antarctica. They live from the equator to the polar north. Some live in dense tropical forests. Some soar high above deserts and some over grasslands. Others choose sea coasts, tundra, or mountain habitats.

The lives and habits of many eagles are not well known. Eagles are often hard to find. Once found, their movements are hard to track. They travel long distances to hunt and to migrate. Most eagles nest in out-of-the-way places.

Scientists think that about 18 of the 59 species are threatened with extinction, because of loss of their habitats.

In Greek mythology, the eagle was the messenger of Zeus, King of the Gods. Only the eagle could grasp lightning without being harmed. That was why the eagle was called Thunderbird.

The 59 species of eagles are divided into four groups. Here are a few examples from each group:

Booted or "True" Eagles

Booted, or "True," Eagles are found throughout the world. Their legs are feathered to the toes, so they look as if they are wearing feathery trousers. They eat small birds, mammals, and **carrion** (already dead animals). A carcass of a Steppe Eagle, *Aquila rapax*, was found on Mount Everest at 24,600 feet (about 4 ½ miles [7,500 meters] up!), which shows how high eagles can fly.

Golden Eagle
Aquila chrysaetos
This eagle is the most common and well-known eagle worldwide. One of its nicknames in North America is Jackrabbit Eagle.

Black Hawk-eagle
Spizaetus tyrannus
This eagle is quite small and weighs between 2 and 2 ½ pounds. It has a broad crest on its head. Seen from below, the wings have black and white patterns that seem to whirl.

Wedge-tailed Eagle
Aquila audax
The Wedge-tailed Eagle, the largest Australian bird of prey, hunts on the dry savannas (grasslands). It is known to feed on wallabies as big as itself!

Fish and Sea Eagles

Fish and Sea Eagles are found everywhere except South America. As you might guess by the name, they are mostly found along shores of oceans, lakes, and rivers. They feed mainly, but not only, on fish. You could call them "pirates," for they steal fish that other birds catch. They also scavenge.

Bald Eagle
Haliaeetus leucocephalus
Is this eagle really bald? No! Its head has plenty of feathers. The name comes from an Old English word *balde* (bal-duh), meaning shining white.

Steller's Sea Eagle
Haliaeetus pelagicus
This eagle lives along rocky seashores, feeding on large fish, crabs, seabirds, and young seals. It occasionally visits islands off Alaska. It makes gruff barking sounds.

Vulturine Fish Eagle
Gypohierax angolensis
This eagle is also called the Palm-nut Eagle. It is the only eagle that eats plants. Besides eating crabs and fish, it "preys" on palm nuts and fruit!

Harpy, or Buteonine Eagles

Harpy, or Buteonine, Eagles live in the tropical forests of South America, Mexico, the Philippines, and New Guinea. Most of them are large with fancy crests. Their wings are short and broad, which helps them maneuver (steer) among close-growing trees. They eat large mammals.

Philippine Eagle
Pithecophaga jeffreyi
Sometimes called the Great Philippine eagle, this is the rarest eagle—almost extinct. In the past many were collected for zoos. Now the loss of forest habitat on the tropical islands where this very large eagle lives endangers it.

Harpy Eagle
Harpia harpyja

The Harpy is the world's most powerful eagle. It is as big as a large turkey and was called "the winged wolf" by the Aztec people. It eats monkeys, sloths, and other tree-dwelling mammals.

Snake, or Serpent Eagles

Snake, or Serpent, Eagles live in tropical grasslands and forests of Africa, Australia, Asia, and Europe. Their legs are short, strong, and unfeathered. They have thick scales. These eagles feed mostly on snakes, even poisonous ones, and the scales offer protection against venomous snake bites.

Bateleur
Terthopius ecaudatus
"Ecaudatus" means "without tail," but this eagle does have a short one! Its feathers, which are red, black, and white, were prized by African tribes for use in their ceremonies and rituals.

Crested Serpent Eagle
Spilornis cheela
This small eagle eats reptiles, tree snakes, and lizards. It opens its wings to make a large target to distract a striking snake. It can digest venom.

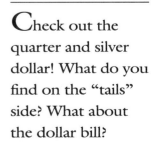
Check out the quarter and silver dollar! What do you find on the "tails" side? What about the dollar bill?

23

The Skies Belong to Eagles Map

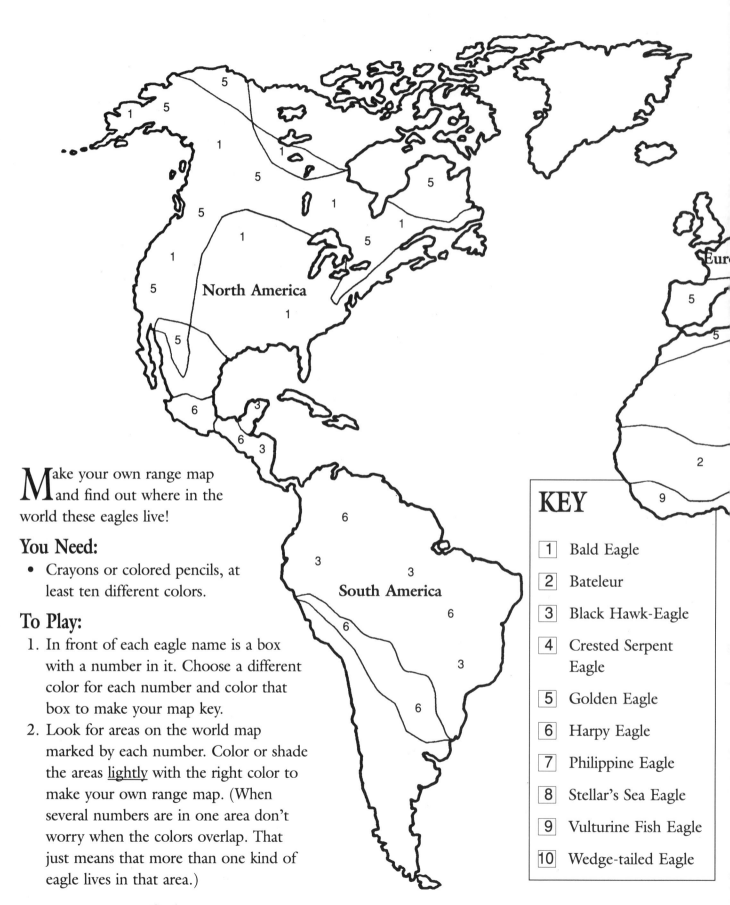

North America

South America

Eur

KEY

1 Bald Eagle

2 Bateleur

3 Black Hawk-Eagle

4 Crested Serpent Eagle

5 Golden Eagle

6 Harpy Eagle

7 Philippine Eagle

8 Stellar's Sea Eagle

9 Vulturine Fish Eagle

10 Wedge-tailed Eagle

Make your own range map and find out where in the world these eagles live!

You Need:
- Crayons or colored pencils, at least ten different colors.

To Play:
1. In front of each eagle name is a box with a number in it. Choose a different color for each number and color that box to make your map key.
2. Look for areas on the world map marked by each number. Color or shade the areas <u>lightly</u> with the right color to make your own range map. (When several numbers are in one area don't worry when the colors overlap. That just means that more than one kind of eagle lives in that area.)

5

5

5

8

8

8

5

5

Asia

5

5

4

5

5

Africa

4

4

2

4

2

4

4

10

2

9

2

10

Australia

10

2

The Bald Eagle is the national bird of the United States. It appears on the Great Seal, holding an olive branch in one talon and a bundle of arrows in the other. The branch and the arrows symbolize the power vested in Congress to make peace and war.

Riders of the Wind

Everyone knows that an eagle is a bird. But what makes it a bird? Flight? Eggs? Feathers?

It's not flight. Flying is not special to birds. Insects and bats also take to the air. Ostriches, emus, kiwis, and penguins are all birds, but they are grounded! They have remnant wings that can't get them airborne, though penguins' wings come in handy as paddles.

It's not eggs. Insects, fish, frogs, toads, snakes, turtles, and even some Australian mammals all lay eggs.

Did you guess feathers? They are the only feature unique to birds, and they are ideal structures for flight.

The central support of a feather is called the **shaft.** The flat area is the **blade.** The blade is made of **barbs** linked together to make an air-resistant surface. (If you find a feather, experiment with pulling the blade apart. What happens? Can you smooth it together again? How?)

The barbs are held together by tiny **barbules,** some with hooks and some with loops, that stick to each other like velcro.

Altogether, a Bald Eagle has about 7,000 feathers. Can you imagine counting them? They weigh approximately $1\frac{1}{2}$ pounds; that's about $\frac{1}{8}$ th of the weight of the bird.

Flight feathers and tail feathers are strong.

Contour feathers are smaller and softer than flight feathers. They overlap to give the bird a streamlined shape.

Down feathers are fluffy. They provide insulation by trapping air next to the body.

In eagles, some of the primaries, the strong wingtip feathers attached to the wrist and finger bones, are narrowed at the tips. When the feathers fit together this creates slots in the wing tips that help to control flight. By adjusting its wing-tip slots and its tail, an eagle can keep on a level, steady course while watching the ground below with a hunter's eyes.

barb

barbule

shaft

blade

26

Birds must groom to keep their feathers fit for flying and insulation. The eagle pulls feathers through its beak to straighten the barbules and to dislodge dirt or parasites. The bird also works oil into the feathers to keep them waterproof. The oil comes from a special preen gland near the tail.

In spite of preening, feathers become tattered and bedraggled. Each year the eagle grows new ones, but not all at once. As old feathers fall out, they are replaced evenly on both sides so that the eagle remains balanced and can always fly.

How does flight work? Wings have a blade-like shape, rounded on top and flatter below. The leading edges are thicker than the trailing edges. This causes air to move faster over the top of the wings and provides the lift that keeps the bird up. (The same principle is used in designing airplanes.) The outer halves of the wings act as propellers to move the bird forward. Tuckable legs—a retractable undercarriage—and sleek feathers help the streamlining. The tail is used for steering and braking. When a bird lands, it moves its wings forward, fans its tail, and extends its feet. It has a special **alula**, or small wing at the wrist, that helps control takeoff and landing.

Eagles flap their wings on takeoff, but once airborne, they spend most of their time gliding or soaring (which takes less energy than flapping).

When an eagle glides, it coasts down and uses the weight of its body to push through the air.

When an eagle soars, wings outstretched and quite still, it is riding rising air currents.

Neil Armstrong, the U.S. astronaut, landed the first manned vehicle on the moon with the words, "The Eagle has landed."

Obstruction Currents

When a steady wind meets a line of cliffs or range of mountains, an updraft forms. Eagles can soar on these updrafts, often traveling along the face of the cliffs for miles.

Thermals

When air over open ground warms up, it rises in columns called thermals. An eagle that rides a strong thermal will rise in a great spiral. In a weaker thermal, the air may rise more slowly than the bird's weight making it lose height. So heavier birds don't start their hunting until the sun has had a chance to warm the ground and create strong thermals. Eagles are not "early birds!"

An eagle can glide down out of one thermal and pick up the next thermal before losing too much height. This is important for long cross-country journeys.

Thermals are often found near storm clouds. It is thought that eagles use clouds as visual thermal-markers. Perhaps that's why the Golden Eagle earned the nickname Thunderbird.

How Fast is an Eagle?

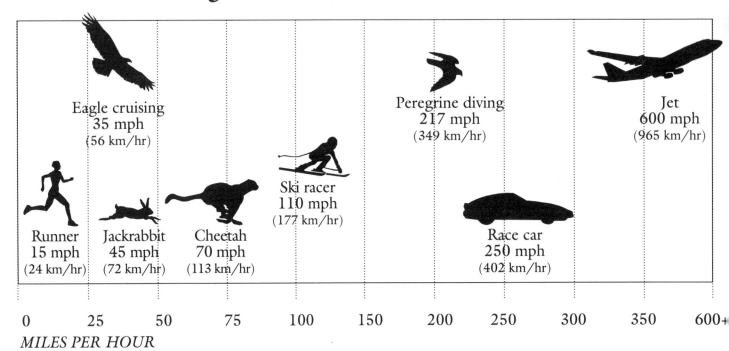

Eagle cruising
35 mph
(56 km/hr)

Runner
15 mph
(24 km/hr)

Jackrabbit
45 mph
(72 km/hr)

Cheetah
70 mph
(113 km/hr)

Ski racer
110 mph
(177 km/hr)

Peregrine diving
217 mph
(349 km/hr)

Race car
250 mph
(402 km/hr)

Jet
600 mph
(965 km/hr)

| 0 | 25 | 50 | 75 | 100 | 150 | 200 | 250 | 300 | 350 | 600+ |

MILES PER HOUR

28

Build an Eagle Wing

A Bald Eagle has a wing span, tip to tip, of up to 7 ½ feet (2.2 meters). Yet an average male Bald Eagle weighs about 9 pounds and an average female weighs about 12 pounds. (Try lifting a 10-pound sack of flour or sugar for comparison.) It is the combination of large wings and light weight that makes the eagles masters of the air.

Build an Eagle Wing Includes:

- Eagle wing pattern on page 31.
- Eagle body on pages 26 and 27.

You Need:

- Crayons, color pencils, or fine tip markers
- Scissors
- Paste or glue
- Two 3/4" brads, also called paper fasteners

Before Assembling:

Cut page 31 out of the book. Color all the pieces. With the eagle wing pattern in front of you, read the following information about eagle flight anatomy. You will be told when to cut out the different pieces and how to assemble the wing step-by-step.

The Bones

The eagle's body, like that of most birds, is designed to be light.

- The whole skeleton weighs less than the feathers!
- Many bones are hollow and porous. They may have struts inside for strength.
- Shoulder, rib, and wing bones are slender.
- The skull is thin, and there are no heavy teeth.
- Birds breathe oxygen from the air. In addition to lungs, birds have extra air sacs that extend into their hollow bones.

They help with breathing. They keep the body light. Air sacs also serve as a cooling system. Flying can be hot work!

1. Cut out the bones from your eagle wing pattern along the dashed lines. Place area A of the **humerus** bone over area A of the **radius** and **ulna** bones and poke through the Xs with a brad. Place area B of the radius and ulna bones over area B of the **carpo-metacarpus** and poke through the Xs with a brad.

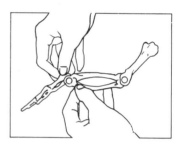

The brads allow movement like the joints of a real wing. Compare the wing skeleton with the diagram of the human arm below.

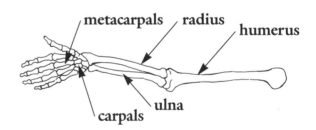

The Muscles

Breast muscles power the wings. If you could look at them, they would be dark in color. That shows they have a good blood supply, pumped by a strong heart, to bring oxygen to working muscles. Chicken breast (white meat) has poor blood supply. That's why chickens do not set long-distance flying records!

2. Cut out the muscles along the dashed lines. Place the muscles over the bones and fold the tabs to the back, matching the symbols. Paste the tabs so that you can lift the muscles up and still see the bones. Part of the humerus bone will still show.

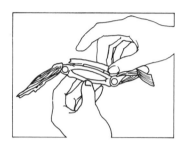

The Feathers

Feathers are made of keratin like your finger nails. They do not grow evenly all over a bird's body, but grow from special cells in feather tracts. (Look at a plucked chicken. Can you see rows of bumps? These mark the feather tracts.) Each cell grows the right kind of feather for that part of the body.

3. Cut out the feathers. Place the wing tip feathers, called the **primaries**, over the bones and muscles first. Note how the feathers fit around the brad. Fold the tabs behind and paste.

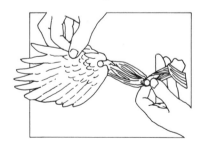

4. Next, place the **secondary** wing feathers over the lower arm muscles and bones. The right side will fit around the brad, and the left side should be allowed to overlap the primary feathers and hide the brad. Fold the tabs behind and paste.

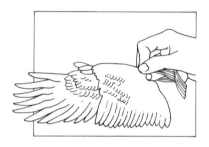

5. The last group of feathers closest to the body are called the **tertials**. Place them over the humerus bone and muscles. Allow the feathers to the left to cover the brad. The breast muscles and humerus bone will still show on the left side. Fold the tab over to the back and paste.

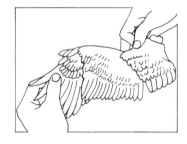

Now the eagle wing is complete. You can lift up the feathers to view the muscles and bones, and the brads allow you to observe how the wing is jointed.

Paste the wing onto the eagle on page 27 by matching area C on the back of the humerus bone to the gray area (C) on the eagle. Notice how the flight muscles attach the breast to the humerus bone. By folding the wing over, it can be enclosed in the book.

Eagle Wing Pattern

Cut out this page, then follow the assembly directions on pages 29 and 30 to build an Eagle wing.

The Bones

The Muscles

The Feathers

Cut here to remove page from book

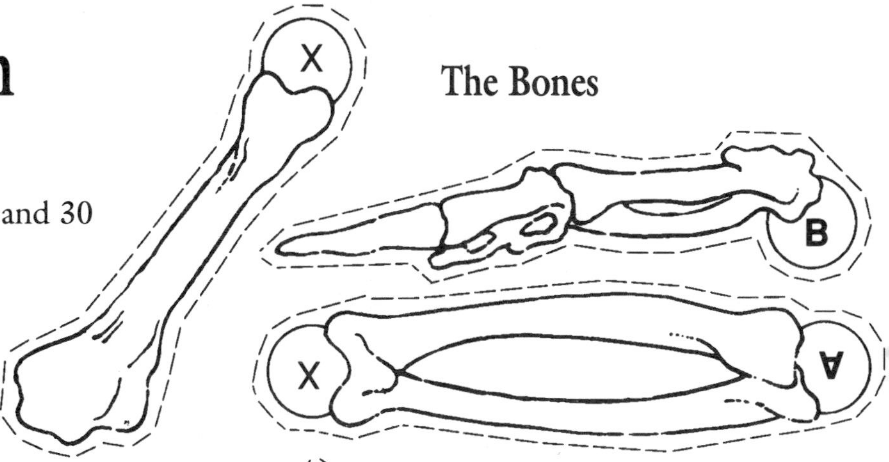

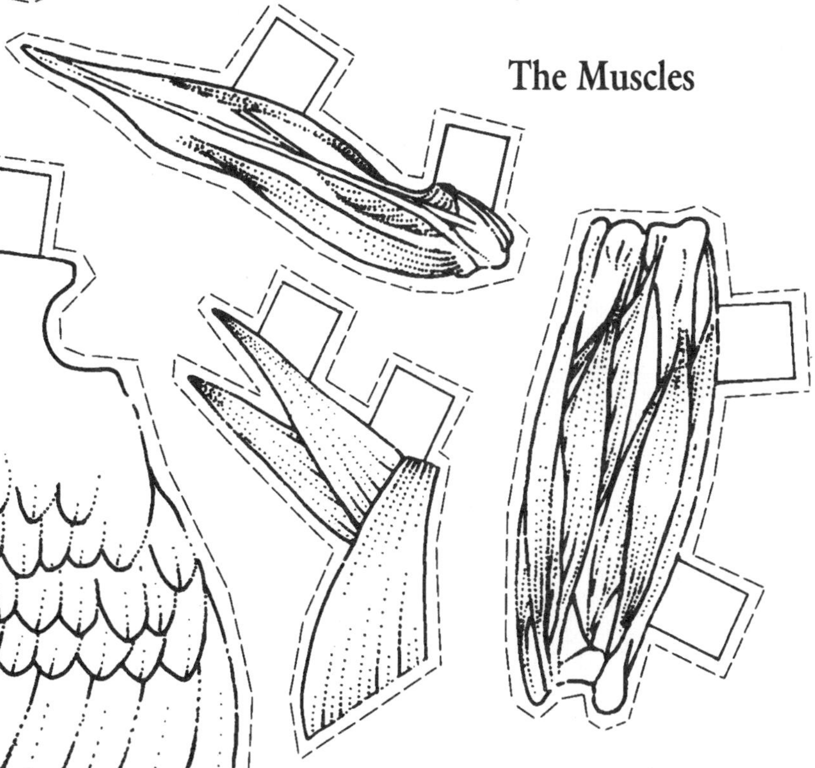

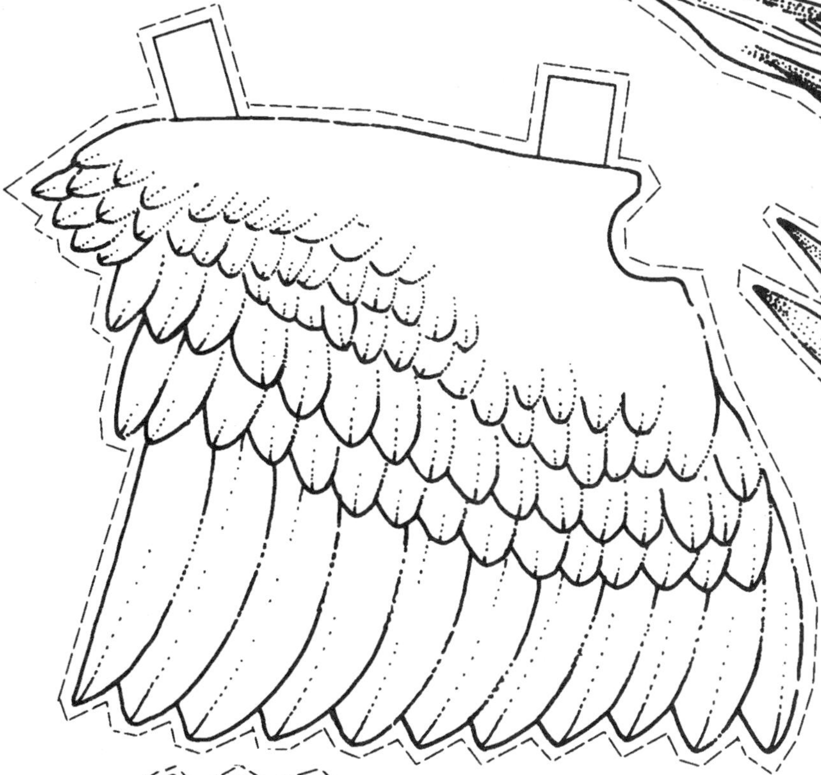

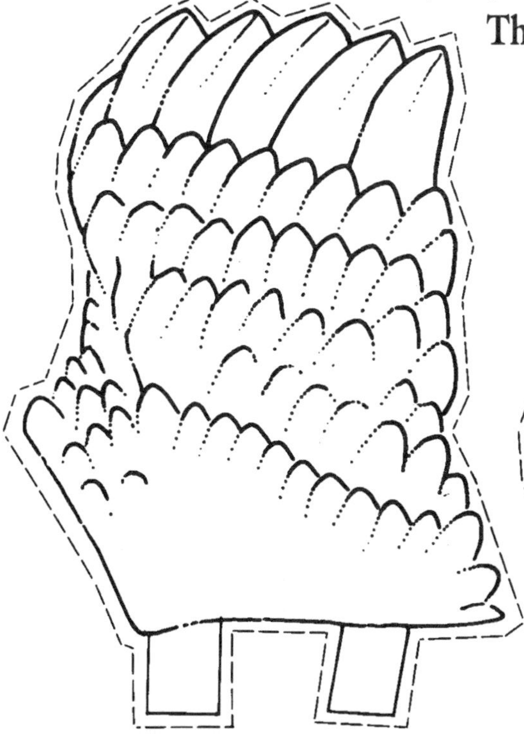

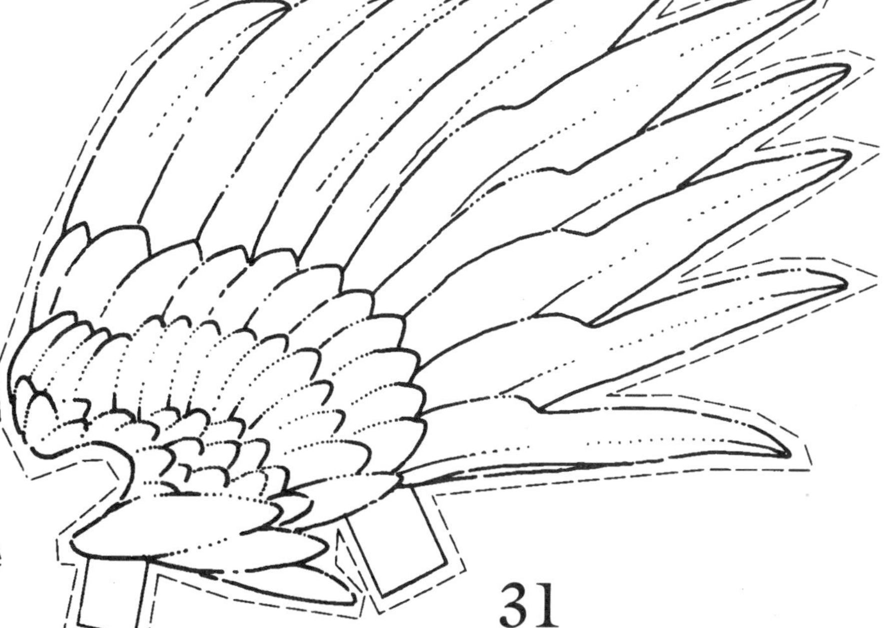

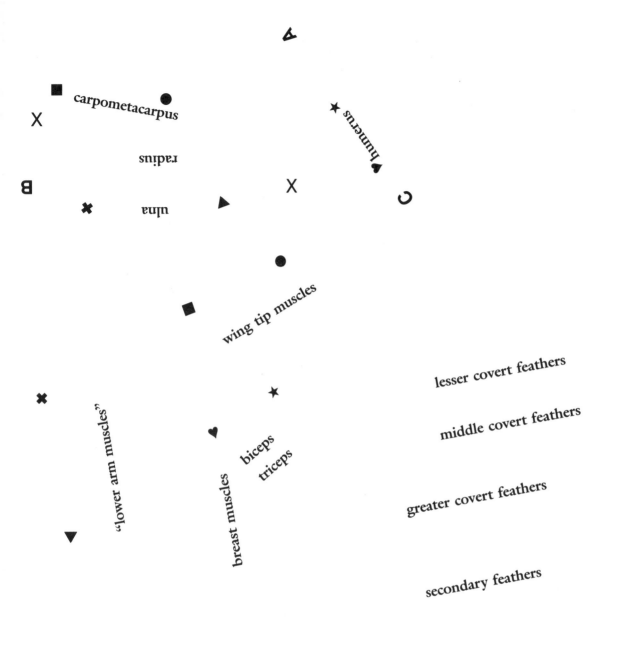

A

■ carpometacarpus ●

X

radius

B

✖ ulna ▲ X C

humerus ★ ♥

●

■

wing tip muscles

lesser covert feathers

middle covert feathers

✖

"lower arm muscles"

♥

biceps

triceps

greater covert feathers

breast muscles

▼

secondary feathers

tertials

primary feathers

greater covert feathers

middle covert feathers

primary covert feathers

lesser covert feathers

alula

On the Hunt

A **predator** (animal that kills other animals for food) that hunts from the air needs more than flying ability and speed. It also needs tools for the hunt—"eagle" eyes and talons.

Eagle Eyes

Eagle eyes are huge compared with the size of the eagle's head. Some eagles have larger eyes than people. The eyes face forward, and the fields-of-view of the two eyes overlap. This is called **binocular** vision. The brain gets slightly different messages from each eye about the same part of the picture. From this, the bird's brain works out distance and speed—important information for a hunter. (Try this for yourself. Hold your finger out in front of you with your arm straight. Then look at your finger first with one eye, then the other. Your finger will appear to jump to the side, showing that each eye sees the picture in a different way.)

Humans blink to keep their eyes moist and clean. Eagles stare intently at an object and seem not to blink. They have a special transparent eyelid, the **nictitating membrane**, which flicks across the eye to keep it moist and clear dust away. This membrane protects the eye from damage when an eagle attacks its prey. It also acts as an anti-glare screen in bright sunlight—like built in shades! The regular eyelids close only when the bird sleeps.

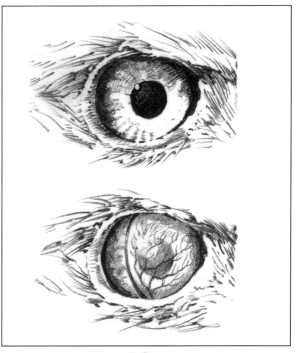
33

Eagles have adorned many postage stamps.

Eagle vision is about eight times sharper than human vision. Eagles scan the ground from high above and can see a rabbit from a mile away. From the same distance humans couldn't even see the rabbit with binoculars.

Are eagles as ferocious as they look? The answer is sometimes, but not always. It's the unblinking stare and the bony, protective ridge above an eagle's eyes that make it look so fierce.

Eagles' ears lie just back from their eyes and are hidden by feathers. Eagles can hear well, but they rely on vision for their hunting.

From the same distance, what can an eagle see that you cannot see?

Eagle's Eye View

You Need:

- Scissors

To Assemble:

1. Cut out the scenery strip below.
2. Cut the dash lines (left) to make slots.
3. Turn the page sideways to read "Eagle's Eye View." Weave the scenery strip first over, then under all the slots. Follow the directions to move the strip so you can see an Eagle's Eye View!

Cover the eagle and observe what a person sees. Cover the person and see the same scene through eagle eyes!

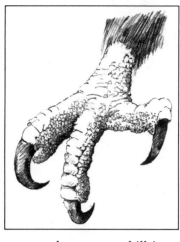

Talons

Once an eagle spots its prey, it has to catch it. That's where talons come in. The first powerful strike from a great height may stun the prey or kill it outright. The eagle uses its strong toes with sharp, curved talons to seize the prey. If the prey is not already dead, the eagle kills it by squeezing and piercing with its powerful talons.

A Bald Eagle's feet are specially adapted to catching fish. The toes have knobbly pads with **spicules** (little spikes) underneath that jab into the slippery prey. The spicules work in the same way that cleats work to keep football players from sliding on grass or mud.

Beaks

Eagles have vicious-looking hooked beaks, but they don't use them to kill their prey. The beaks are used to tear meat or fish. Eagles usually strip away fur or feathers before they devour their prey. Even so, some material is swallowed that can't be digested. This matter is coughed up in pellets. Pellets are sometimes found beneath eagle roosts. The remains of bones, scales, and other animal material in the pellet provide clues about the eagle's diet, but don't tell the whole prey story. When eagles feed on larger mammals or carrion, they tear chunks of flesh that contain very little bony and indigestible matter.

Going Hunting

Golden Eagles hunt over open grasslands and deserts, ever watchful for signs of prey far below. A successful attack depends on surprise. The eagle often cruises along just behind a ridge, checking over the top every so often. If it sees prey, it will swoop down for the kill.

Prey-animals are often **camouflaged**, which means they blend in with their surroundings. Movement catches a predator's eye. If a small animal sees the predator or even the shadow of the predator moving across the landscape, it will "freeze" to avoid giving itself away.

Golden Eagles sometimes hunt in pairs. One eagle, usually the heavier female, walks on the ground to scare up a rabbit while the lighter and swifter male circles above. When the startled rabbit runs to escape the first eagle, it may be caught unaware by a surprise attack from the second one.

A Bald Eagle sometimes glides along shorelines and over marshes, swooping down to catch fish or water birds it happens to see. More often it hunts from a perch overlooking a favorite fishing hole. There it waits and watches until it sees a fish, then glides down and grabs the fish in its talons. Flying can be difficult if the fish is heavy or if it is struggling. If need be, the eagle can swim to shore dragging the fish. It uses its great wings to do a splashing butterfly stroke. Bald Eagles also wade into the water to catch fish or even wait over a hole in the ice. This is one situation in which the eagle might use its curved bill as a killing tool. Bald Eagles steal fish from each other and even hijack Ospreys (fish hawks) in midair to steal their catch.

The Chain of Life

Living things get energy to live and grow from the sun. Because plants have **chlorophyll**, a green pigment, in their leaves they are able to use energy from the sun, water, and carbon dioxide in the air to make food. **Herbivores**, animals that eat plants, get their energy secondhand from plants. They are called primary consumers. They need to eat a lot of plants to get enough energy to survive. Predators hunt and kill animals for their food. They are called secondary consumers. They get their energy third- or fourthhand and need to eat many animals to get enough energy. They are said to be at the top of the **food chain**.

Bald Eagles are at the top of the food chain. They eat more surface-swimming fish than bottom-feeding fish. They take what's easy to see. For this reason, they take dead or dying fish, which float belly-up revealing their silvery undersides. This type of feeding can sometimes harm eagles because of the way the food chain works.

Suppose Bald Eagles hunt fish that are dead or dying because they inhabited polluted waters. The fish fed on insects, plants, or smaller fish that contained poisons. The large fish accumulated poisons that made them sick or killed them. The poisons stay in the fat of the fish-bodies. Eagles that eat the fish, because they are easy to see and catch, also eat the poison. The poison is stored in the fat of the eagle's body. One poisoned meal might not matter. But if the eagles feed on poisonous fish day after day, more and more poisons collect in their fat. The accumulation of poison can make the eagles sick, harm their reproduction, or even kill them.

Test this yourself. Build a Bald Eagle Food Chain Pyramid on these pages, then turn to page 38 for directions to see toxins move through the food chain that you have built.

Build a Food Chain Pyramid

The Food Chain Pyramid will paste into the book on the base below. When the pages are closed, it will fold down, and when the pages are open, you will be able to pull a tab to make it pop up.

Build a Food Chain Pyramid Includes:
- The base, below, on pages 36 and 37.
- The food chain pattern on page 39.

You Need:
- Crayons, color pencils, or fine tip markers
- Scissors
- Paste or glue

Before Assembling:
Color, then cut out the pieces on page 39 following the dashed lines.

The Bald Eagle Food Chain Pyramid

X

To Assemble:

1. First make the eagle pop-up by pasting strips A and B together at right angles and folding as shown.

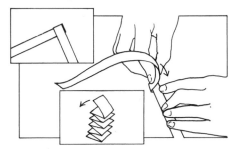

Paste one end of the strips to the X on the back of the eagle, and the other end to the X on page 36.

Pull tab to pop-up

Cut
Slot #2

Cut
Slot #1

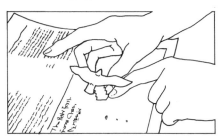

■

◆

▼

2. Fold each layer of the food pyramid in half along the solid lines so the pictures face out. Unfold, opening so the pictures face you. Fold all the tabs back. Paste the three layers of the food pyramid in place by matching the symbols on the bottom tabs to the symbols on pages 36 and 37. In the correct position, the pictures fold face down, then fold in half along the inside of the book when closing the pages.

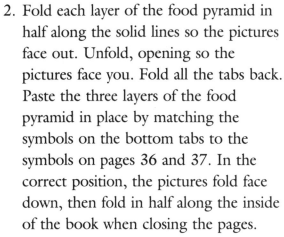

3. Paste the top tab of the plant layer to the small fish layer by matching the Ys. Paste the top tab on the small fish layer to the large fish layer, matching the Zs.

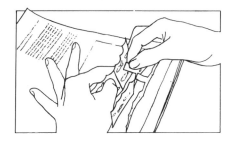

4. Paste strip C to the C on the back of the large fish layer. Cut the slots on page 37 (you may want an adult to help you) and weave the strip through slot #1, going through to page 38, then back out to page 37 through slot #2.

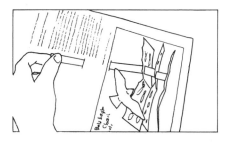

Your Bald Eagle Food Chain Pyramid is now complete! The assembly will fold down easily by laying the three layers picture side down. When you turn the page or close the book, the food pyramid layers will fold over and the eagle will smush down. When you open pages 36 and 37, the eagle will pop-up. You can then pull the long tab on page 37 and the layers will pop-up.

Toxins in the Food Chain

In the food pyramid, what if some plants are toxic. (Draw a red dot on some plants in the first layer of your food chain pyramid.) When a little fish eats the plant, it gets a red dot for every plant it eats. (Draw two red dots on most of the little fish.) When the big fish eats the little fish it gets two red dots for every small fish it eats. (Draw four red dots on every big fish.) Then comes the eagle. What happens to the red dots? Now imagine that every day, all summer (say 90 days), the eagle gets red dots in its food. (Draw them.) How must the eagle feel now?

Scientists look at eagles as **indicators** of the health of an environment. Eagles are among the first to show signs of stress from pollution of any kind because of the way poisons concentrate in their bodies. It may also be easier to notice the effects of pollution in eagles than in less visible animals.

Have You Ever Wondered?

Do eagles carry off human babies?
Stories about eagles carrying off babies are fantasy! Eagles are not strong enough to carry off large animals. Even if they take off from a cliff edge in a favorable wind, they can barely carry their own weight. Normally, when they take off from the ground they can carry at most about 5 pounds.

Do eagles always carry prey away from the kill?
An eagle doesn't always carry its prey away. It may feast where it made the kill. It **mantles** (hides the prey with its wings) if another bird or animal comes close.

How much does an eagle eat?
That depends. Although an eagle will **gorge** (eat enormous amounts quickly) on a fresh kill, it eats less each day in proportion to its weight than do tiny birds. About 1 ½ pounds (one medium cottontail or half a jackrabbit) a day is enough.

Napoleon Bonaparte, who was Emperor of France from 1804 to 1815, used an eagle as his emblem.

Food Chain Pyramid Pattern

Cut out this page, color the pattern pieces, then follow the assembly directions on pages 37 and 38 to build a Bald Eagle food chain pyramid.

Cut here to remove page from book

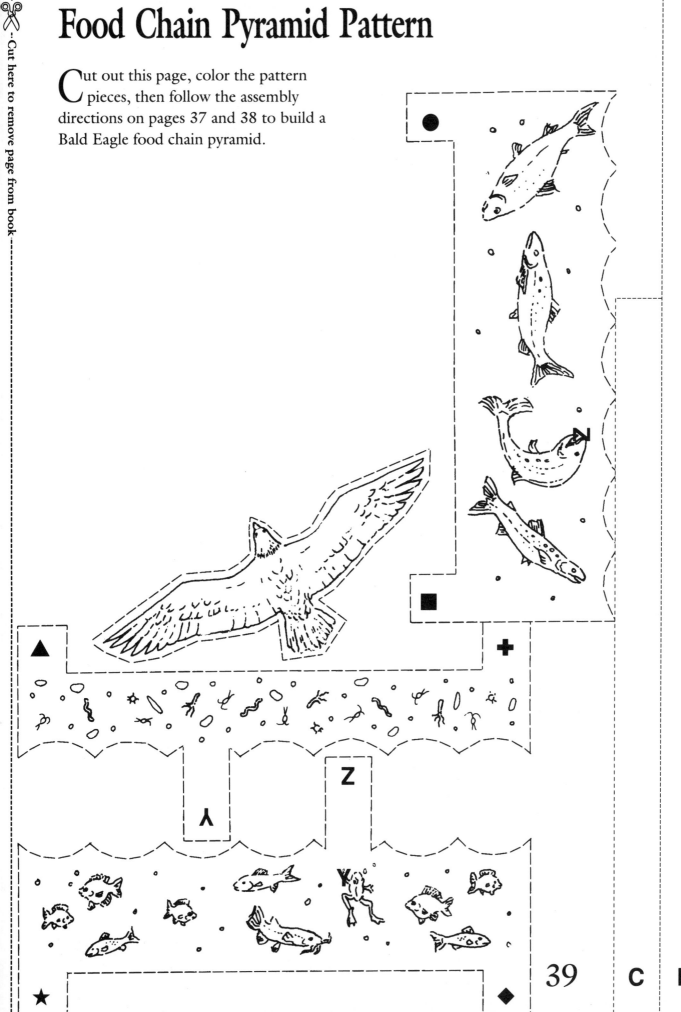

39   C   B   A

FOLD

FOLD

C

X

FOLD

FOLD

FOLD

FOLD

FOLD

FOLD

FOLD

FOLD

40 FOLD

FOLD

Family Affair

An eagle usually stays with the same mate for its entire life. If one of the pair dies, the other will find a new mate. Somewhere within their **home range**, the area over which they hunt, each pair of eagles selects a nest site. Year after year, the eagle pair will return to the same nesting territory. The nests may be in tall trees or on rocky bluffs or cliffs. Eagles defend the area around their nest. They soar above the territory boundaries as if advertising, "This place is taken. Keep out!" Or they fly to and fro over the area with looping flights. They will chase and harass intruders to keep them away from the nest.

Eagle nests are large and get bigger each year as the eagles add more sticks to them. They may be up to ten feet (3 meters) across. One record-breaking nest was 20 feet (6 meters) high before it became so heavy it broke the tree in which it was built. The nests are lined with soft moss or lichens.

Golden Eagles may have several nests within their territory. Each year they select one nest to use. No one is quite sure why the eagles choose one nest over another. They may use them in turn, so that each year they have a nest that is free of parasites. They may choose the nest that is snow-free. They bring green pine twigs to the nest, too. No one knows why. One theory is that resin in the twigs keeps bugs away.

Some Golden Eagle nests have other nests in them. These "nests in nests" belong to pack rats or small birds. Strange as it may seem, the smaller creatures are usually safe from the eagles. The eagles can't catch them because the small creatures live in the sides of the nest. The eagles can only land on the top, which provides a flat landing platform.

Some Alaskan Bald Eagles build nests on sea stacks—the rock pillars standing in the ocean—and cliffs along rocky shores. This is because many coastal areas of Alaska have no trees.

The family life of eagles is a story in itself. Scientists know how eagles live because they spend many hours watching eagles' nests. The observers take notes on each happening: courtship, the changing shifts of the adult as they sit on the eggs, the hatching of the eggs, the feeding of the young, and so on. No detail is too small to be important. Pieced together, these details tell the whole story of the day-to-day life of eagle families.

The Eagle Family Album

Make your own book, *The Eagle Family Album*, so you can learn about the family life of eagles. Follow the assembly directions below.

The Eagle Family Album Includes:
- The book pattern on pages 43 and 44.
- The pictures on page 45.
- The key on page 64 to check your work.

You Need:
- Crayons, color pencils, or fine tip markers
- Scissors
- Paste or glue
- Stapler or needle and thread

Before Assembling:
- Cut page 43 out of the book. <u>Do not</u> cut the other dashed lines yet!

How to Assemble The Eagle Family Album

1. Place page 44 in front of you so that the page numbers 2 and 11 are upright.

2. Fold the three bottom panels up along the solid line. Pages 4 and 9 should be upright.

3. Fold top panels down along solid line. Pages 6 and 7 should be upright.

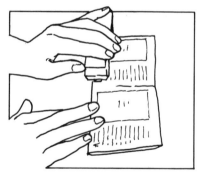

4. Fold book in half along center solid line. Page 1 should be in front, page 12 in back. Open to pages 6 and 7 in the center and staple or sew along the solid center line to bind your book.

5. Close the book with page 1 in front. Cut through all the pages following the dashed lines at the top and bottom of page 1. Now you can read the story!

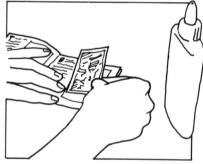

6. Color and cut out the pictures from page 45 and paste into your book on the page that explains it best. You now have a fully illustrated Eagle Family Album!

7

New eaglets are grayish white and fuzzy, and so wobbly they cannot stand. They hatch in the order the eggs were laid— several days apart. The first eaglet grows even before the second eaglet hatches.

9

After about five weeks in the egg, the first eaglet hatches. It uses a special egg tooth, a small spike near the beak tip, to break the tough shell. It's a long, tiring task that can take as long as two days.

12

The eaglets learn to hunt on prey that's easy to catch (often carrion). At first, they don't hunt over water. They steal food when they can. In late summer they leave their parents for life on their own.

1

The Eagle Family Album

Events in the Life of a Bald Eagle Family

6

By eight weeks, the eaglets have grown brown or brown and white feathers. Their beaks and talons are well developed. They can stand and walk around. They tear at food the parents bring.

4

The female eagle lays two or three eggs, two to four days apart. The eggs are dull white. The female begins **incubating** (sitting on her egg) as soon as the first egg is laid.

While the female incubates the eggs, the male hunts for food. The female turns the eggs regularly, using her beak. The male egg-sits, too. They trade places carefully, minding their huge claws!

The male hunts for food to bring to the eaglets. The female tears small morsels of food and feeds the eaglets from her beak. The first-hatched gets more than its share because it is bigger!

Spiral flights, talon-locking, and "kek, kek, kek" cries are all part of courtship. Displays strengthen the bond between the male and female eagle. After courtship, the eagles mate.

At 11 to 12 weeks of age, the eaglets leave the nest. The first flight may be from one branch to another, from one tree to another, or a long glide to the ground. Landings are often clumsy.

Eagles add to their huge stick nests year after year. The nests are lined with moss, pine needles, grass, or feathers. The eagles bring green branches to the nest, too. No one knows why.

One eaglet preens. The other flaps its wings to strengthen them and leaps in the air and drops to the nest again—flying practice. They play-attack their food, testing their hunting skills.

The Eagle Family Album Pictures

The pictures below tell the story of an eagle family, but they are out of order. To put them in the correct order, read *The Eagle Family Album* after you have assembled it. Color, then cut out these pictures and paste each one on the page that explains it <u>best</u>. Do the cover last. Now you have the whole story!

Field Guide to Eagles

John James Audubon, the famous artist and **ornithologist** (person who studies birds), drew portraits of the eagles of North America at a time when the birds were first being given scientific names. He drew a Bald Eagle with a white head and tail. And he drew a large dark bird he called Washington's Eagle. He didn't know at the time that they were the adult and immature of the same species.

Immature eagles look quite different from adults. Each **molt** (period of shedding feathers) changes the color of the plumage a little. By the time a Bald Eagle is four to five years old, it has a white head and tail—the sign of adulthood. At this time Bald Eagles are sexually mature and first breed.

The pictures will help you to recognize eagles in the wild—if you get a good look at them. Sometimes, all you see is a shape against the sky or a hunched shape on a pole or tree. Then you have to guess by shape. Here are some silhouettes of various birds, including eagles, to practice on.

The wingspan and body size of the eagles are marked on the field guides. But can you picture how big they really are?

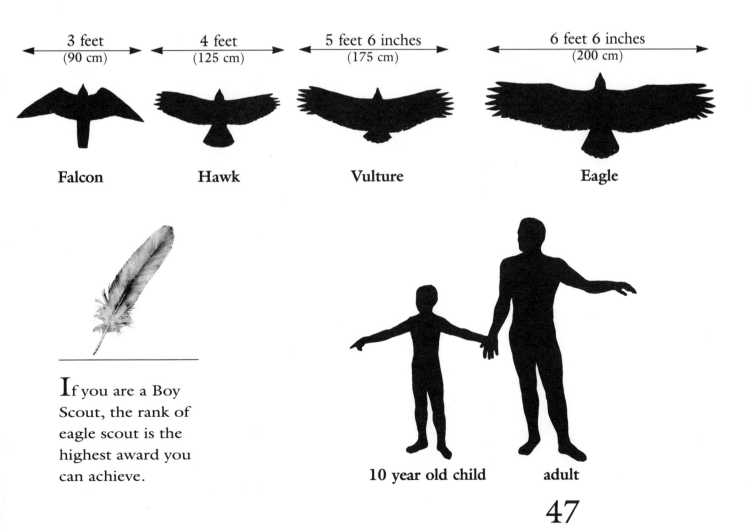

3 feet (90 cm)	4 feet (125 cm)	5 feet 6 inches (175 cm)	6 feet 6 inches (200 cm)
Falcon	Hawk	Vulture	Eagle

If you are a Boy Scout, the rank of eagle scout is the highest award you can achieve.

10 year old child   adult

47

On the Move

Some Bald Eagles live in the same area year round. They are known as **residents**. They are able to find food there summer and winter.

Other eagles spend their summers in the far north. There they find enough food to sustain them. They nest and raise their families. But northern winters are hard. Before the harsh winter sets in, freezing the lakes and covering the land with snow, the eagles must move to the coast or far to the south, where they are still able to hunt.

These journeys are full of dangers, but the eagles have no other option. They must move with the food supply.

Scientists have put very light radio transmitters on some eagles' tails. The instruments don't interfere with movement. (An eagle has even been seen preening its antenna as if it were another tail feather!) The radio beeps allow the scientists to track all journeys the marked eagle makes.

Some eagle nestlings are fitted with bands on their legs. If the birds are later found, dead or alive, that provides information about the travels of that bird.

Some eagles at the Snake River Birds of Prey Area in Idaho nest on the special platforms put up on the high-voltage towers by the power company. They are safer on the platforms than they would be if they tried to nest near the electrical cables.

Did You Know...

- Some young eagles migrate in reverse. They are ready to fly from their nests in Florida early in the year. They spend the rest of the summer traveling north to Chesapeake Bay and up to Canada.
- Breeding Bald Eagles defend their nests. Outside of breeding season, eagles gather where there is a good food supply. They feed and roost together. They don't defend a territory, though they may squabble over food.
- At the Chilkat Bald Eagle Preserve, near Haines, Alaska, up to 4,000 Bald Eagles gather in fall to feast on dead and dying salmon. The Chilkat River has warm springs that keep it flowing long after the surrounding areas are locked in the deep freeze of winter. Salmon travel up the river to spawn. Then they die. The Bald Eagles make the most of the feasting.
- Up to 100 Bald Eagles migrate from Canada to spend the winter at the Rocky Mountain Arsenal near Denver, Colorado. The arsenal is not near a large area of water and there is no supply of fish and water birds. The eagles live on prairie dogs, which are abundant on the grasslands. The Bald Eagles share the hunting in this refuge with Golden Eagles, Ferruginous Hawks, Red-tailed Hawks, and Rough-legged Hawks. The eagles share communal roosts in large cottonwood trees. Why is this wintering ground so unusual? See page 57.

The Migration Game

Could you make it from your wintering ground to your nesting territory if you had to overcome the dangers of migration?

The Migration Game Includes:
- The game board (pages 50 and 51)
- Eagle playing pieces (page 53)
- Eagle cards (page 53)
- Nesting tokens (page 53)
- Numbered squares (page 53)

You Need:
- Crayons, color pencils, or fine tip markers
- Scissors
- Paste or glue

Objective:
To be the first eagle or pair of eagles to arrive in the far northern nesting grounds with six nesting tokens.

Before Playing:
1. First cut page 53 out of the book. Cut out the nesting tokens, the numbered squares, and the eagles ONLY.
2. Color strips A and B red. Color strips C and D blue. Cut out all four strips along the dashed lines (do not cut the solid lines).
3. Fold along the solid lines on each strip with the colored sides facing out. Match the letter (A, B, C, or D) to the X on the uncolored side and paste.
4. Paste an eagle onto each of the bases you just made by matching the dot under the eagle to the dot on top of the base.
5. Cut out the Eagle Cards, shuffle and place TRUE/FALSE side down.
6. On the game board (page 51), cut along the dashed lines on either side of the bridge to make two slots. Slide the pile of cards under the bridge on the game board.
7. Place the nesting tokens in the nest on the game board.
8. Put the numbered squares in a lunch bag, envelope, or cup.
9. Read the directions for play on page 50.
10. Pick a number. The highest number goes first.

Aztec Knights of the Eagle wore costumes of eagle feathers. Their rivals were the Knights of the Jaguar. In mock battles, the eagles represented light and the jaguars darkness, or the war between day and night, or good and evil.

Directions:

For two or four players.

1. Place your eagle to start on SOUTH. Draw a number and move in either direction. If playing as pairs, alternate turns: you go first, opponent second; your partner third, your opponent's partner fourth. Continue to move forward in the direction you began.

2. When you land on a space with arrows, you may, on your next turn, choose to move in any direction shown, allowing you to take shortcuts or change direction. If there is only one arrow, you must move in that direction.

3. If you take a shortcut and land on a THERMAL space, move your eagle to the triple arrow space. On your next turn, choose your direction.

4. When you land on a question space (?), your opponent(s) draw an Eagle Card from under the bridge and read the statement out loud from the category shown on the question space. You must answer True or False. (You may confer with your partner.) If you answer correctly, collect 1 nesting token. If incorrect, your opponent(s) reads the correct answer out loud.

5. Once you (or you and your partner together) have six nesting tokens, you must advance to the NORTH NESTING GROUNDS. If, on your way, you lose a token, you must continue playing until you have six again.

6. To enter the nesting grounds, an eagle must land on the triple arrow space. On the next move, the eagle may advance north. You must land on, or move past, the corner marked NORTH NESTING GROUNDS to win. If playing as pairs, both eagles must arrive to win.

50

The Migration Game

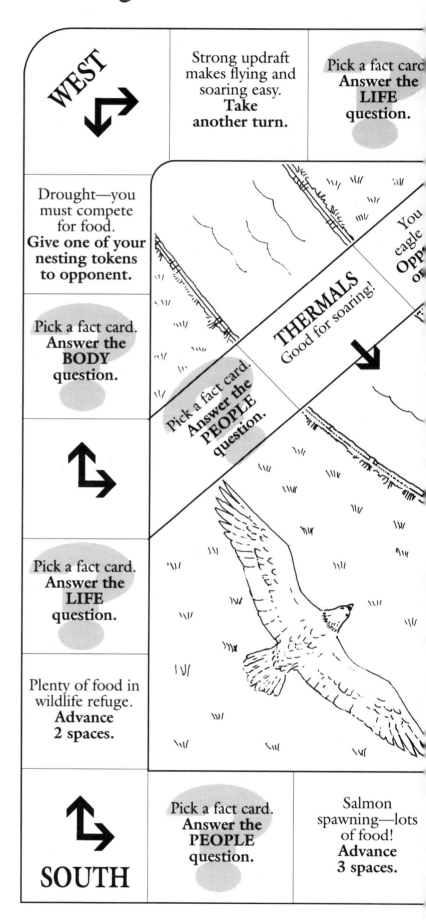

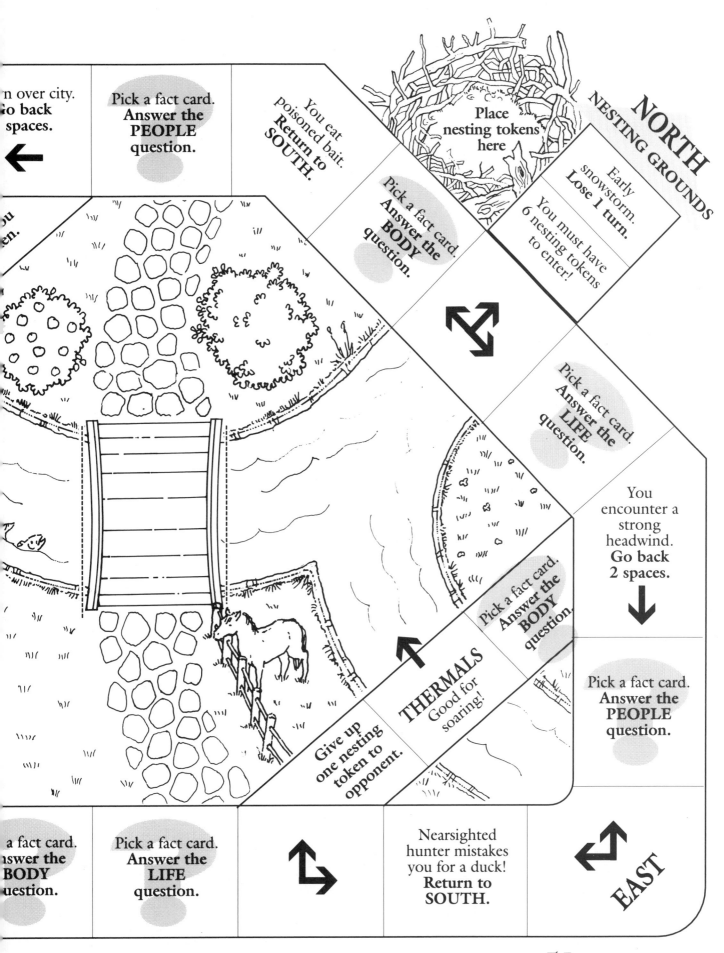

n over city.
Go back
spaces.

Pick a fact card. **Answer the PEOPLE question.**

You eat poisoned bait. **Return to SOUTH.**

Place nesting tokens here

Early snowstorm. **Lose 1 turn.**

You must have 6 nesting tokens to enter!

Pick a fact card. **Answer the BODY question.**

Pick a fact card. **Answer the LIFE question.**

You encounter a strong headwind. **Go back 2 spaces.**

Pick a fact card. **Answer the BODY question.**

Pick a fact card. **Answer the PEOPLE question.**

THERMALS Good for soaring!

Give up one nesting token to opponent.

a fact card. swer the **BODY question.**

Pick a fact card. **Answer the LIFE question.**

Nearsighted hunter mistakes you for a duck! **Return to SOUTH.**

EAST

51

To Play Again:

Save your playing pieces, Eagle Cards, nesting tokens, and numbered squares in this book! Place them into an envelope and tape or paste the envelope to this page.

Old Abe, a Bald Eagle, went to war. He became the mascot of the 8th Wisconsin Regiment during the Civil War. He survived many battles, though he lost some tail feathers at the Battle of Corinth. After the war, the soldiers nicknamed him "our bald-headed veteran."

Eagle Cards and Playing Pieces

BODY
An eagle has about 700 feathers.

PEOPLE
Lead makes eagle feathers glossy.

LIFE
Eaglets in a nest hatch at the same time.

BODY
Eagle bones are solid to make them strong.

PEOPLE
Eagles can digest most poisons without harm.

LIFE
Eagles usually have 1 or 2 young.

BODY
All Golden Eagles have gold-colored feathers.

PEOPLE
Cutting rain forests makes more space for eagles.

LIFE
Eagles make new nests every year.

BODY
Bald Eagles have no feathers on their heads.

PEOPLE
Power lines make good eagle perches.

LIFE
Young eagles drink milk.

BODY
Primary feathers are used for flying.

PEOPLE
People cause more harm to eagles than other predators.

LIFE
Eagles hatch with all their feathers.

BODY
Down feathers keep birds warm.

PEOPLE
Most eagles die of old age.

LIFE
Eagles need large territories.

BODY
Eagles weigh about the same as first graders.

PEOPLE
All eagles in the U.S. are protected under law.

LIFE
Golden Eagles nest on cliffs.

BODY
Eagles rub oil on their feathers when they preen.

PEOPLE
Eagles adapt well to city life.

LIFE
Eaglets practice flying by flapping wings.

BODY
Eagles have three eyelids on each eye.

PEOPLE
Philippine Eagles are endangered.

LIFE
Bald Eagles can't fly until one year old.

BODY
Eagles see 100 times better than humans.

PEOPLE
The Endangered Species Act protects Bald Eagles.

LIFE
Bald Eagles always eat fish.

BODY
An eaglet pecks out of its egg using an egg tooth.

PEOPLE
The Golden Eagle is the U.S. national bird.

LIFE
Eagles track their prey by smell.

BODY
Harpy Eagles make noises like harp music.

PEOPLE
Eagles can carry off human babies.

LIFE
All eagles are predators.

BODY
Serpent Eagles have feathery legs.

PEOPLE
Native Americans value eagle feathers.

LIFE
Eagles never eat food they have not killed.

BODY
Eagle beaks are designed to kill prey.

PEOPLE
Mexico has a flag with an eagle on it.

LIFE
Eagles hunt at dawn and dusk.

BODY
Booted Eagles have legs covered in rubber.

PEOPLE
The U.S. Post Office uses an eagle symbol.

LIFE
Golden Eagle flocks hunt large mammals.

BODY
Eagles can digest every scrap of their prey.

PEOPLE
Columbus brought eagles to America.

LIFE
Antarctic Eagles hunt penguins.

BODY
Eagles grow new feathers to replace worn ones.

PEOPLE
Eagles are so common, they are easy to study.

LIFE
Bald Eagles are found all over the world.

A		●
B		●
C		●
D		●

1	**2**	**3**	**4**	**5**	**6**

Nesting tokens

BODY TRUE	BODY FALSE	BODY FALSE	BODY FALSE	BODY FALSE
	Their heads are covered with white feathers.	Only <u>adult</u> Golden Eagles have them.	Eagles have light, hollow bones.	An eagle has about 7,000 feathers.
PEOPLE TRUE	**PEOPLE FALSE**	**PEOPLE FALSE**	**PEOPLE FALSE**	**PEOPLE FALSE**
	Eagles can be electrocuted by power lines.	It destroys habitat that some eagles need.	Poisons make eagles sick and can kill them.	Lead is toxic to eagles and can kill them.
LIFE FALSE	**LIFE FALSE**	**LIFE FALSE**	**LIFE TRUE**	**LIFE FALSE**
They have fuzzy down.	They eat bits of meat or fish.	They reuse nests for many years.		The first egg laid hatches first.

BODY FALSE	BODY TRUE	BODY TRUE	BODY FALSE	BODY TRUE
Eagles see about 8 times better than people.			The largest eagles weigh less than 20 pounds.	
PEOPLE TRUE	**PEOPLE TRUE**	**PEOPLE FALSE**	**PEOPLE TRUE**	**PEOPLE FALSE**
		Eagles need wide open spaces.		Many eagles die from accidents, shooting, traps, or toxins.
LIFE FALSE	**LIFE FALSE**	**LIFE TRUE**	**LIFE TRUE**	**LIFE TRUE**
They eat small mammals and birds.	They fly at 2 to 3 months old.			

BODY FALSE	BODY FALSE	BODY FALSE	BODY FALSE	BODY TRUE
Booted eagles have feathered legs.	Talons kill prey, beaks tear flesh apart.	Their legs are scaly to protect them from snake bites.	The name "Harpy" means witch-like.	
PEOPLE TRUE	**PEOPLE TRUE**	**PEOPLE TRUE**	**PEOPLE FALSE**	**PEOPLE FALSE**
			This is a myth, or story.	The Bald Eagle is our national bird.
LIFE FALSE	**LIFE FALSE**	**LIFE FALSE**	**LIFE TRUE**	**LIFE FALSE**
Golden Eagles don't gather in flocks.	They hunt in daytime.	Eagles scavenge carrion (dead animals).		Eagles rely on vision for hunting.

X

X

X

X

6 5 4 3 2 1

BODY TRUE	BODY FALSE
	Bits of fur, bones and feathers are cast as pellets.
PEOPLE FALSE	**PEOPLE FALSE**
Eagles are difficult to study, and most are rare.	Eagles were here long before people.
LIFE FALSE	**LIFE FALSE**
They are exclusive to North America.	There are no eagles in the antarctic.

Eagles and People

We know from fossils that the oldest eagle was a booted eagle that lived 36,000,000 years ago. Since then, eagles have roamed the skies freely. Their greatest threats were extremes of weather or starvation when prey was scarce. Some eggs or nestlings were eaten by predators. Some young birds fell from the nest or crashed on their first flight. But the hazards were all natural…

until people came on the scene. We became the eagles' greatest threat.

At one time, people believed all predators were cruel and evil. Hunters were paid bounties for killing them. Many predators, including hundreds of thousands of eagles, were killed.

We know now that predators play an important role in nature. They help keep nature in balance. Without predators, prey animals would increase in numbers until there were too many for the land to support. Soon there would be no food left for them. Some animals would starve to death. Others would die of diseases that spread more easily when animals are crowded together. Predators help to control prey populations by catching the weakest, sickest, or oldest animals. The fit animals are more likely to escape. The result is a healthier population.

Eagles are no longer shot for bounties. We understand their value as predators. For more than fifty years eagles have been protected by the law, and the laws were made stronger when the Bald Eagle was recognized as an **endangered** species (in danger of becoming **extinct**). But over the years, even since we enacted laws to protect eagles, we have hurt them in many hidden ways.

Pollution Problem

A chemical called DDT was invented to kill mosquitos that carried disease. DDT did what it was designed to do all too well. Besides killing mosquitos, it killed all the other insects that were sprayed. Many small birds that fed on DDT-contaminated insects also died. The remains of DDT last a long time in the ecosystem.

Charles Broley, an enthusiastic birder, began to band Bald Eagles in Florida in 1939. He was studying their migration and behavior. He banded eaglets year after year. As the years passed, he noticed fewer young in each nest. More nests failed to produce eaglets. By 1957, most nests hatched no young. Gradually Broley and other scientists pieced information together. The DDT caused the birds' eggs to have thin and fragile shells. A mere touch, let alone the effort of a parent trying to incubate the eggs, was enough to smash them. Charles Broley worked very hard to convince people to pass laws to ban DDT. In 1972, the United States banned DDT; Canada banned it in 1985.

Another deadly danger for Bald Eagles is the lead shot used for duck hunting. Injured ducks, full of toxic pellets, are easy pickings for the eagles. But all that lead can make an eagle sick or even kill it. People are not allowed to use lead shot for duck hunting any longer. But lead pellets left in the environment don't rot away. They go on being a danger for years.

Golden Eagles survived DDT better than Bald Eagles. Their food was less often contaminated with toxic sprays. But Golden Eagles faced other threats. Thousands were shot in the 1940s because ranchers called them lamb-killers. (They do eat carrion and occasionally kill weak and injured lambs, but they have never been the "evil" birds that ranchers believed them to be.) Illegal shooting still takes place. Eagles still die from eating poisoned bait put out for coyotes. They still die in leghold traps put out to catch fur-bearing mammals.

Eagle populations do not recover quickly after they are harmed by DDT, lead, or other hazards. In a healthy environment, eagles live long lives. They are not mature enough to breed until they are four to five years old. Eagle families are small, and eagles do not breed every year. So it takes many generations to rebuild a population, even in ideal conditions.

Bald Eagles are making a comeback. But they are still endangered in many of the lower 48 states and threatened in the rest. Are we winning for eagles? Only time will tell.

Pollution Solution

The Rocky Mountain Arsenal is an unusual place: it is within a city, near a major airport, surrounded by busy highways, and yet it provides eagles with a refuge. It became a haven for wildlife because it offered open space in the middle of a city and very few people entered the area.

Entry to the Arsenal is controlled because some parts of the Arsenal are badly polluted and dangerous. For many years, highly toxic chemicals were made there. That stopped long ago. Now the area is being cleaned up. At the same time, scientists are studying the way the eagles use the habitat. It is important to know in detail what the eagles eat, how they behave, where they come from, and how long they stay.

The scientists also make sure that prey animals do not stray into areas that are still contaminated with chemicals. If rabbits or prairie dogs were to eat vegetation that contained toxic chemicals they would be a danger to hunting eagles because poisons concentrate at the top of a food chain.

The arsenal clean-up is being done carefully, so it does not disrupt the eagles or destroy the habitat they need. No one is sure if the arsenal can ever be completely free of toxic chemicals, but it is important that we try to reduce the pollution to a level that will not harm eagles and other animals. We owe it to wildlife. And we owe it to ourselves not to give up on even an inch of our planet. It's the only home all living things—people, too—will ever have. In a way, the arsenal is both a test of how well we can restore the land and a symbol of our resolve to do right by wildlife, just as the Bald Eagle is a symbol of pride in our country.

In Imperial Rome, when Julius Caesar led the armies, each Roman legion (a unit of soldiers) had a standard. The standard was a silver or gold eagle within a wreath of victory mounted on a pole.

Help for Hurt Eagles

Just like Shining One in the story, sick and injured eagles need special care to help them get better and stay wild. The goal is for them to fly free. Sigrid Ueblacker knows that reaching that goal takes skill, hard work, and a lot of caring. With the help of her volunteers, Mrs. Ueblacker has cared for more than 120 eagles at her raptor hospital in Colorado. She has also looked after thousands of other falcons, hawks, and owls.

Mrs. Ueblacker didn't plan to work with wildlife. One day one of her four children came home with an injured starling. Mrs. Ueblacker tried her best to help the bird. She knew how much it meant to her daughter. The starling survived. People in the neighborhood began to bring injured and orphaned wildlife to Mrs. Ueblacker for care. She seemed to have a way with animals, with her soft voice and calming touch. It was work she loved to do. It was not long before she got her wildlife license.

Mrs. Ueblacker's home was soon full of hurt birds. She decided it was time the birds had their own space. So she started the Birds of Prey Rehabilitation Foundation in Broomfield, Colorado. The foundation is one of a network of licensed raptor hospitals throughout the country.

With her own family grown, Mrs. Ueblacker works long hours caring for her ever-changing family of injured raptors. She spends time talking to people about the eagles she helps at the hospital. She believes that if people learn more about raptors, they will work to protect and save them.

Ask Mrs. Ueblacker

How do you learn to help eagles?

Mrs. Ueblacker reads all the books she can find about looking after injured wildlife. She talks to other wildlife rehabilitators about the way they care for birds. They compare notes and share ideas. She tries different methods of care to see what works best.

"The longer I deal with raptors, the more I learn about them," she says. "They suffer so much at the hands of people. I have special sympathy for them."

How do eagles get hurt?

Some are shot. Mrs. Ueblacker remembers one eagle peppered with more than 50 BBs. Some are injured in traps. Others fly into power lines or vehicles, or suffer from lead poisoning from eating contaminated food. One eagle arrived fighting for breath and with claws tightly clenched. It died from the toxins in its body.

The modern country of Mexico has an eagle on its flag and coat of arms.

How are eagles cared for?

Mrs. Ueblacker works closely with a veterinarian to decide on treatment and medicines for the birds. An injured bird stays in intensive care until it shows signs of reviving and begins to eat and keep down its food. The first solid food it gets is often a tender baby rat or a piece of rabbit. Later, Mrs. Ueblacker moves the eagles into large flight cages where there's wing-spreading room. The shady and airy cages are made of wooden slats that are smooth and safe. The cages, among the largest in the country, are 108 feet (33 meters) long (that's longer than a basketball court), 25 feet (8 meters) wide, and 18 feet (5 meters) high.

"One day, I shall have cages three times that long," Mrs. Ueblacker says. There, in the large enclosures, the eagles fly from perch to perch. Their flight muscles become strong. They catch their own live food—rabbits, rats, and quail.

How are eagles kept wild?

After an eagle moves into the flight cage it has almost no contact with people. It learns to be wild again by being with other eagles. Mrs. Ueblacker watches from day to day to see how well it flies and hunts. All eagles have to "graduate" flying and hunting before they are set free in good eagle territory.

What is a typical hospital day like?

There is no such thing as a typical day. Mrs. Ueblacker is always ready to change plans to deal with an emergency. But the jobs get done somehow. The birds are fed. The cages are cleaned. The rodent house (where mice and rats are raised to feed the raptors) is cleaned. There may be trips to the vet. Mrs. Ueblacker has volunteers to help with the work. She always takes time to check that her birds are eating properly and recovering well.

Are all eagles at the center injured?

No. Some of the eagles at the hospital are just young and orphaned. Mrs. Ueblacker takes care of them until they have strong flight feathers and can catch their own food. Then they are released in the winter of their first year into a communal roost area. The young birds then pick up survival techniques from the adult eagles.

Where are birds released?

When it is possible, adult birds are released in the area from which they came. The eagles may be transported to Nebraska or Utah if they were found there. One long-distance traveler came from Alaska for flight rehabilitation in the long flight enclosure. After "graduating" flight, it returned to Alaska. (No, it didn't fly, it went by airplane!) One eagle was released at the Rocky Mountain Arsenal during Prairie Dog Appreciation Day.

"After all," Mrs. Ueblacker says, "who can appreciate prairie dogs better than an eagle?"

What if an eagle fails hunting and flying tests?

An eagle may seem healthy, but may not be able to fly strongly enough to hunt. It would never survive in the wild. Mrs. Ueblacker may keep it as a foster-parent bird. If it gets **broody** (behavior that shows it wants to nest), it is used to care for, and teach, an orphan eagle. The young eagle learns to hunt and learns that it is an eagle—it doesn't get used to people. Other unreleasable birds are used to teach people the importance of predators. Perhaps one has visited your school?

Do all the eagles survive?

Sadly, some eagles are so desperately injured or sick that they die. Some must be **euthanized** (put to death painlessly) because they could never again hunt or fly—and for an eagle, life without the freedom of the air is no life at all.

In ancient Egyptian hieroglyphs, the letter A is the figure of an eagle.

Choose for Eagles

Would you make the right decisions for eagles? Try the "Choose for Eagles" challenge. Circle the answer you think are right, then check page 62. Are you a hot shot, a ho-hum, or a hazard?

1. You find a Bald Eagle's nest at a lake near your home. Would you:
   a) Get as close as you could to see if the nest had young?
   b) Keep away, and tell wildlife officials so they could safely monitor the nest?
   c) Tell your friends so you could all go throw rocks at it?

2. Your neighbor is about to tip antifreeze from his car into a storm drain. He says, "I'll pour it where pets can't lick it—it's poisonous." Would you:
   a) Ask your neighbor not to pour poisons into the storm drain (even if it is to keep it away from pets), because poisons flow into the rivers and harm fish and other wildlife?
   b) Paint a luminous pink sign on the curb: DUMP YOUR ANTIFREEZE HERE.
   c) Tell your Dad so he can dump his old automobile oil in the drain?

3. Your family moves into a new house. The people before you left a shelf full of pesticides, which your family does not want. Would you:
   a) Offer to help Mom by flushing the pesticides down the sink and throwing the empty bottles in the trash?
   b) Junk the bottles into the trash without opening them?
   c) Store the bottles in a locked closet until you find out how your town deals with toxic waste safely?

4. You see a wounded Golden Eagle by the side of a road. Would you:
   a) Wrap it in wet newspaper to keep it cool?
   b) Leave it alone because it will probably die anyway?
   c) Notify the U.S. Fish and Wildlife Service, or other wildlife officials, so they can take the eagle to a wildlife vet?

What You Can Do to Help Eagles

1. Learn as much as you can about their lives, their needs, and their world—this book is only a beginning.
2. Get your friends and family excited about eagles, too.
3. Speak up for eagles. If development threatens a wildlife area you know, write a letter to your newspaper about it. Let everyone know you care.
4. Get your school class, your nature club, or your neighborhood to support an eagle research or rehabilitation center if there is one near you.

The Last Word

Long before there were any people, there were eagles. Mighty hunters, they soared through the air and claimed the bounty of the land. They shared the vast wild spaces with pronghorn and prairie dogs, bison and beetles, and a million other living things. The dangers they faced were natural ones—an early freeze, a late thaw, a violent storm.

Today, fewer eagles share the earth with masses of people. Billions of us build and live in vast cities. Our freeways and power lines slice across eagle habitat. Our smoke and fumes dirty the air. Our toxic wastes spill into rivers, streams, and groundwater, contaminating every level of life. The greatest dangers eagles face are caused by people.

The Sioux people believe that all plants and animals are part of the great circle of life. Everything that crawls, slithers, or gallops over the prairie; everything that burrows in the soil, everything that soars or flutters in the bright sky, has its rights. Eagles, elk, earthworms, and people all have their place.

Can we adopt this ideal? Can we make the world safe for eagles, for all creatures? Can we prevent the circle of life from breaking?

That depends on all of us…

Choose For Eagles Answers

Give yourself 5 points for each correct answer.

1b) If you know that eagles nest, roost, or hunt in an area, stay away. Eagles don't like humans crowding them.

2a) Your neighbor was smart to think about pets being harmed by antifreeze. He or she should also understand that poison that gets into a storm drain can end up in our groundwater, streams, or rivers. It can harm wildlife throughout the food chain.

3c) Pesticides are highly toxic in water and in landfills. Some towns and cities have collection days for toxic household waste, so that it can be disposed of safely. If your town doesn't do this, perhaps it's time it did. This would be a good neighborhood campaign!

4c) Although Grandfather and Gil in the story helped the eagle, you should never try to help an eagle. Even injured eagles are powerful and may hurt someone not trained to handle them. Many injured eagles *can* be helped if wildlife officials are told about them in time. So report injured eagles to your local wildlife agency, to the United States Fish and Wildlife Service, or to your local Humane Society.

Scoring:

20   Definitely a hot shot and a friend to eagles. Well done!

15-10   Not bad, but not great—ho-hum for eagles. Will you get 20 next time?

5-0   Eagles, watch out—here comes an eagle hazard! Will you ace the quiz next time?

Glossary

alula (AL-yuh-luh)—cluster of feathers on the thumb of a bird that forms a small wing to help control flight

barb (BAHRB)—the strands of a feather that together make the blade

barbules (BAHR-byools)—small hooks and loops that lock the barbs of a feather into a smooth blade

binocular (beye-NAHK-yuh-luhr)—a kind of vision in which both eyes see the same scene so the animal can judge distance and speed

blade (BLAYD)—the broad flat part of a feather

broody (BROOD-ee)—sitting on eggs and caring for young

carrion (KAR-ee-uhn)—dead and decaying animal flesh

chlorophyll (KLOHR-uh-fihl)—green pigment in plant cells needed for the plant to make food from sunlight

communal (kuh-MYOON-uhl)—feeding or roosting area used by groups of birds

contour feather (KAHN-tur FETH-uhr)—an outer feather that helps to streamline body shape

diurnal (deye-UHRN-uhl)—active in the daytime

down feather (DAUN FETH-uhr)—a soft feather that insulates a bird from cold

endangered (ihn-DAYN-juhrd)—at risk of becoming extinct

euthanize (YOO-thun-neyez)—to put to death painlessly

extinct (ik-STIHNKT)—animal or plant species that has died out everywhere in the world

family (FAM-uh-lee)—in classification, a category that includes similar genera

food chain (FOOD chayn)—the linkage of the sun, plants, and animals through their food and energy use

genus (JEE-nuhs) (plural **genera** [JEN-eh-reh])—group made up of similar species

gorge (GOHRG)—to eat a large amount all at once

herbivore (UHR-buh-vohr)—animal that eats plants

home range (HOHM RAYNJ)—the whole area used by eagles for hunting

incubate (IHN-kyuh-bayt)—sit on eggs and hatch them by the warmth of the body

indicator (IHN-duh-kayt-uhr)—an animal whose presence and condition is used to judge the health of a habitat

mantle (MANT-uhl)—to shield dead prey with outstretched wings during feeding

molt (MOHLT)—to shed feathers before growing new ones

nictitating membrane (NIK-tuh-tayt-ihng MEHM-brayn)—transparent third eyelid of a bird's eye that cleans and protects the eyeball (from a Latin word meaning "wink")

ornithologist (awr-nuh-THAHL-uh-juhst)—person who studies birds

predator (PRED-uht-uhr)—animal that hunts and kills other animals for food

preen (PREEN)—to straighten feathers with the bill

raptor (RAP-tuhr)—bird of prey

resident (REZ-uhd-uhnt)—bird that lives in the same area all year

shaft (SHAFT)—the strong center support of a feather

species (SPEE-sheez)—set of animals that are grouped together for classification because they are alike and can interbreed

spicule (SPIK-yool)—a small spike

stoop (STOOP)—very swift dive through the air from a great height

territory (ter-uh-TOHR-ee)—the area an eagle defends against intruders

Bibliography

Bailey, Jill. 1988. *Birds of Prey*. Nature Watch Series. Facts on File Publications, New York and Oxford.*

Bancroft-Hunt, Norman and Werner Forman. 1981. *Indians of the Great Plains*. Orbis Publishing Ltd., London.

Birnie, David. 1988. *Birds*. Eyewitness Books. Alfred A. Knopf, New York.*

Gordon, David G. 1991. *The Audubon Society Field Guide to the Bald Eagle*. Sasquatch Books, Seattle.

Johnsgard, Paul A. 1990. *Hawks, Eagles, and Falcons of North America*. Smithsonian Institution Press, Washington and London.

Lang, Aubrey. 1990. *Eagles*. Sierra Club Wildlife Library. Little, Brown & Co., Boston, Toronto, and London.*

Lindop, Edmund. 1966. *War Eagle, The Story of a Civil War Mascot*. Little, Brown & Co., Boston and Toronto.*

Newton, Ian (editor). 1990. *Birds of Prey*. Facts on File. New York, Oxford, and Sydney.

Patent, Dorothy Hinshaw. 1984. *Where Bald Eagles Gather*. Clarion Books. Ticknor & Fields (Houghton Mifflin Company), New York.*

Ryden, Hope. 1985. *America's Bald Eagle*. G. P. Putnam's Sons, New York.*

Sattler, Helen Roney. 1989. *The Book of Eagles*. Lothrop, Lee & Shephard (William Morrow & Co. Inc.), New York.*

Savage, Candace. 1987. *Eagles of North America*. Northword Press, Inc., Minocqua, Wisconsin.

Terres, John K. 1980. *The Audubon Society Encyclopedia of North American Birds*. Alfred A. Knopf, New York.

Yellow Robe, Rosebud. 1979. *Tonweya and the Eagles and Other Lakota Indian Tales*. Dial Press, New York.*

Video: 1991. *Spirit of the Eagle*. Miramar Production.

* These books are of interest to younger readers.

The Denver Museum of Natural History appreciates the encouragement, time, and support of the following:

Project Sponsor—U.S. Department of the Army
Cooperating Agencies—U.S. Fish and Wildlife Service, National Fish and Wildlife Foundation
Publication Coordinator—Betsy R. Armstrong
Technical and Educational Review—Dr. Charles Preston, Joyce Herold, and Diana Lee Crew, Denver Museum of Natural History; Carol Ann Moorhead, U.S. Fish and Wildlife Service
Design—Gail Kohler Opsahl
Illustration—Marjorie C. Leggitt and Gail Kohler Opsahl
Cover Illustration—Marjorie C. Leggitt

Production Art—J. Keith Abernathy and Gretchen Kingsley
Thanks to Alana Berland, Katie Duffy, Whitney Frick, Jessica Harvey, Colin Hudon, Jennifer and Jeremy Kamlett, Heidi Lit, Adele Martin, Joe and Matt McConaty, Erik Robins, Paige Stapp, Chad Spurway, and Susan Lipstein's class from Hackberry Elementary School, who tested the activities.

Design Motif—geometric pattern on cover is based on a traditional Sioux beadwork design.